TECH EQUITY

FREEDOM THROUGH ENABLING TECHNOLOGY

A Dream Officer's Playbook for Tech Equity in Disability & Aging Services

By

Precious "Preciosa" Myers-Brown

Chief Innovation and Dream Officer (CINO)

The Voice of Enabling Technology™

House of CINO

Copyright

Publisher's Note & Disclaimers

This book is provided for educational and informational purposes only and does not constitute legal, medical, clinical, regulatory, or financial advice. Readers should consult qualified professionals and applicable federal, state, and local guidance before implementing policies, programs, or technology solutions.

Some stories are shared from the author's lived experience in the field. To protect privacy, certain names, identifying details, and contextual elements may be changed or generalized.

All product names, logos, and brands mentioned in this book are property of their respective owners. Any references are for identification or commentary purposes and do not imply endorsement.

Dedication

For my grandmother, Francena Brown Hicks,
who left her home to give me options,
and taught me that freedom is worth fighting for.
I got you, Grandma. I got you.

HOW TO USE THIS BOOK

This book was written for everyone who believes people deserve more than survival.

Whether you're a state director shaping policy, a provider CEO running an agency, a DSP on the front lines, a family member fighting for your loved one, or a person receiving services who wants more from life, this book is for you.

But before we go any further, let me tell you who I am.

I am a spiritual person. My foundation is God. You will feel that throughout this book, and you will definitely feel it in Chapter 12. I don't separate my faith from my work because my work IS my faith in action. When I talk about purpose, when I talk about calling, when I talk about why I do what I do, it comes from that place.

If you submit to the universe, to a higher power, to divine purpose, to something bigger than yourself, you'll understand what I mean. If that's not your framework, I still invite you to stay. The principles are universal, even if my language is rooted in my own spiritual tradition. The lessons about dignity, freedom, and human-centered care apply to everyone, regardless of what you call the source.

I say this now so you're not surprised later. In my presentations, I frame it upfront and people lean in. I want to give you the same courtesy here. When you get to Chapter 12 and you feel the shift, you'll understand. That's where my whole self shows up.

Now, let me help you navigate.

If you're a STATE DIRECTOR or POLICYMAKER:

Start with Chapter 10 (Policy, Funding & Leadership Blueprint). Then read Chapter 11 (Building the Next System). These chapters give you the language, the ROI data, and the implementation roadmap you need.

If you're a PROVIDER CEO or AGENCY LEADER:

Start with Chapter 9 (When Systems Fail) to see what's at stake. Then read Chapter 11 (Building the Next System) for your transformation roadmap. Come back to Chapter 5 (The Frameworks) when you're ready to train your teams.

If you're a DIRECT SUPPORT PROFESSIONAL:

Start with Chapter 7 (The Future Workforce). You'll see yourself in these pages. Then read Chapter 6 (Smart Supports) to understand how technology makes your job better, not obsolete.

If you're a FAMILY MEMBER:

Start with Chapter 8 (Aging in Place). Then read Chapter 5 (The Frameworks), especially The Seven Freedoms. These will give you language to advocate for what your loved one deserves.

If you're a PERSON RECEIVING SERVICES:

Start wherever you want. This book was written for you first. But if I had to choose, I'd say start with the Opening Chapter. My grandmother's story is your story too, the fight for freedom, dignity, and choice.

If you want the full journey:

Start at the beginning. Read it cover to cover. Let the stories build. Let the frameworks sink in. Let the vision take shape.

However you read this book, know this:

You are not alone.

There is a movement building, people across this country who believe that enabling technology, when done right, can restore freedom, protect dignity, and transform care.

And now you're part of it.

Welcome.

Let's build the future together.

Precious "Preciosa" Myers-Brown

Chief Innovation and Dream Officer (CINO)

The Voice of Enabling Technology™

Contents

OPENING CHAPTER: PART I

THE WOMAN WHO TAUGHT ME FREEDOM

I was raised by a woman who stood no taller than four-foot-nine, but whose presence made grown men straighten their backs when she walked into a room. She wasn't loud. She didn't need to be. Her voice had that low, Southern-sweet tone that carried more history than volume, soft enough to soothe you, but firm enough to stop you mid-sentence when necessary. And when she didn't want to speak on a thing, she hummed. Lord, that hum. A soft little Negro spiritual that let you know she had thoughts... she just chose peace.

Her name was **Francena Brown Hicks**, and she came from the red soil of **Barnwell, South Carolina**, born into a segregated South that offered Black folks a life boxed in by boundaries they did not create. Yet somehow, with nothing but faith and a dream that refused to die, she tore those boundaries down with her bare hands.

She used to tell me, "I left home to give you options."

And she meant that.

When she left Barnwell, left her mother, her cousins, her entire community, she wasn't leaving because she wanted to. She was leaving because the world she deserved wasn't available where she was born. So she and my grandfather packed up their courage, their cotton-grown resilience, and their God, and headed north to Harlem.

Harlem became the place where she learned to walk with purpose. South Carolina made her strong, and Harlem made her unstoppable.

Before the post office, she drove a New York City taxi, the yellow and black ones with the dome and the fold-down seats. A 4'9" woman navigating Manhattan traffic like she owned every block. Everyone who knew her before I came along called her a spitfire. And from what I saw, they weren't wrong.

She was an avid bowler, an Eastern Star member, and played the organ at Antioch Baptist Church in Queens. This tiny woman contained multitudes.

She worked at the post office at **JFK Airport**, tossing boxes off mail planes like she had the body of a linebacker instead of a tiny Disney character. She would drive the tractor trailer all around the airport, delivering shipments wherever they needed to go. Even when people joked she had a "Mickey Mouse voice," she'd just hum and keep working, moving with a speed and precision people twice her size couldn't match.

Then she'd clock out, go home, sleep a little, and wake up before dawn to cook dinner for the entire house. Morning light, frying pans, and gospel humming, that's where the real conversations happened. The kitchen wasn't just where she fed us. It's where she **formed** us.

"Precious," she'd tell me, sliding a pot onto the stove with that little wrist twist only church women and Southern aunties have mastered, **"you can do bad all by yourself."**

It wasn't an insult. It was empowerment wrapped in a warning. A reminder that I didn't need to tie my future to anyone else's limitations. That I had options she never had. That God gave me gifts I was expected to use.

She was traditional in some ways, modern in others. She taught me how to be a wife and how to run a household, but she also made it very clear that I was born to live big, to lead, to think for myself. She didn't raise me to shrink.

And that balance, heritage and freedom, tradition and liberation, is the foundation of who I am today.

But as she got older, and her body began to betray the strength she'd carried through decades of sacrifice, something shifted in our relationship. I saw the fear in her eyes, not fear of death, but fear of losing control. The fear of becoming "a burden." The fear of being placed in a system she didn't trust.

One day, during one of our morning conversations, she looked at me with all seriousness and said:

"If you put me in a nursing home or you leave me, I will haunt you for the rest of your life."

And the thing is... we all knew she could. That woman's spirit was strong enough to pull it off.

She said it jokingly, maybe, but with her, all jokes came wrapped in truth. Under that threat was a plea wrapped in love: **"Don't let them** take my freedom from me."

That moment was the spark that lit the fire inside me.

It was the moment I realized something I had never articulated before. People aren't afraid of aging. People are afraid of losing power, dignity, choice, connection. My grandmother wasn't scared of her body changing. She was scared of a system deciding her future for her.

That day, over the smell of frying onions and the familiar hum of a spiritual she didn't even realize she was humming, I made a silent promise to her:

I will not let the world take your freedom. And I will not let it take anyone else's either.

What I didn't know then was that this promise would become the foundation of my entire career.

And then came the mice.

Yes, the mice.

I know that doesn't sound profound, but let me tell you something. Revolutions don't always start with grand moments. Sometimes they start with tiny intruders you can hear but can't see.

Something happened in the house next door that caused a sudden mouse problem. My grandmother tried to handle it herself because she handled everything herself. But when she admitted it was "too much this time," I saw an opportunity, not for pest control, but for innovation.

I bought every electronic sensor and remote trap I could find. I installed them throughout the house. I set up remote alerts on my end. I gave her wireless call buttons so she could reach me from anywhere.

And for the first time in my life, I saw what technology could really do. It could support without suffocating. It could protect without taking over. It could empower without replacing human love.

That moment, standing in her house, solving a real problem with simple tech, became the first chapter in my life's purpose.

I didn't call it "enabling technology" then. I didn't call it "remote supports." I didn't call it "digital transformation." I called it **love in action**. I called it **keeping my grandmother safe**. I called it **protecting her freedom**.

And I didn't know it at the time, but I was witnessing the very thing this book is about: **Technology, when designed with humanity at the center, becomes liberation.**

That is why I fight so fiercely for tech equity today.

Because I watched a Black woman from the segregated South claw her way toward freedom, and I refuse, REFUSE, to let systems steal from others what my grandmother traveled hundreds of miles to claim: choice, dignity, safety, connection, a life with options.

This book is not just about devices or data or dashboards. This book is about **freedom**, and how technology, when done right, can help sustain it.

My grandmother left Barnwell for better options. I entered this work to protect them.

OPENING CHAPTER: PART II

THE PROMISE THAT BECAME MY PURPOSE

I didn't know it then, but that moment with the mice wasn't just a funny family story or a crisis we managed on the fly. It was the birthplace of a shift, a widening of the lens I had already been looking through for years.

Because I need to make something clear. I didn't enter the disability field because of my grandmother. I was already there. This field raised me. I started working in disability services at **fourteen years old**. Yes, fourteen. I grew up in this work. This wasn't a career path I stumbled into. It became my first calling.

By the time I was in her kitchen, installing sensors and remote alerts, I had already spent years advocating for people's dignity, autonomy, and right to live a full life. I had already seen how systems could restrict people. I had already been the one pushing for more freedom, more choice, more possibility.

My grandmother didn't introduce me to advocacy. She expanded it. She refined it. She sharpened it. She made it personal in a way that shifted my entire approach.

See, traditionally, we used assistive technology and durable medical equipment, big communication devices like the old Dynavox, adaptive switches, the tools that helped people move, speak, express, and communicate. Those were familiar. They were part of the field.

But the moment I set up those electronic traps, those call buttons, those remote alerts in her home, something different happened inside me. I saw technology not just as equipment, but as **freedom**. I saw it not as a device, but as a **bridge** between safety and independence.

I started asking myself questions I had never asked before. If this could help her stay free, who else could we be freeing? Who else was losing autonomy because the system lacked imagination? Who else wanted privacy but couldn't get it? Who else wanted the dignity of living on their own terms? Who else could thrive if we stopped letting outdated regulations shrink their possibilities?

I realized something we don't say enough. The problem isn't that people don't want independence. **The problem is that the system doesn't know how to support it.** And technology, when used right, gives us a new map.

After that moment with my grandmother, I began to see everyone differently. I saw the adult who just wants to sleep through the night without staff entering their room. The elder who wants to stay in their own home, in their own smell, on their own pillow. The young person with a disability who wants alone time. The aging parent who wants peace without sacrificing autonomy. The caregiver who wants to support without suffocating. The agency leader who wants to innovate but is trapped by red tape.

I started seeing the gaps, gaps I had lived with for years, through a new lens.

My grandmother didn't ignite my passion for this field. She **evolved** it. She sparked the paradigm shift from "How do we care for people?" to "How do we ensure people remain themselves?"

Because her fear wasn't about aging or dying or needing help. Her fear was about losing *herself*. And that dignity-based, identity-based fear is the same fear I have seen in thousands of people across disability and aging services. The same fear families whisper. The same fear staff witness but don't know how to soften. The same fear that has shaped policies, practices, and narratives for decades.

What happened in her home helped me understand something fundamental. **People aren't afraid of needing support. They're afraid of losing their power.**

And that is where technology becomes transformational, not as a solution, but as a partner. Technology doesn't replace human care. It expands it. Technology doesn't erase relationships. It preserves them. Technology doesn't take away independence. It restores it.

After that experience with her, I stepped back into the disability field differently. I wasn't just supporting people anymore. I was analyzing the system. Questioning it. Pushing it. Reimagining it. I began looking at every limitation and wondering: **"Is this a real barrier, or just a lack of imagination?"**

That is when I began to understand my work in a new way. I wasn't just doing human services. I was doing human freedom work. I wasn't just helping people. I was protecting agency, dignity, choice, and identity. I wasn't just advocating. I was designing a future.

My grandmother's moment didn't start my journey. It **elevated** it to its next dimension. It connected my ancestral purpose to my professional purpose. It connected my cultural roots to my leadership voice. It connected the spiritual legacy she gave me to the innovation legacy I was meant to build.

And that is why I fight for tech equity today. Not for the devices. Not for the dashboards. Not for the funding. Not for compliance. Not even for innovation's sake. But for the thing my grandmother almost lost, the thing she vowed to haunt me over: **Freedom.**

This book is the continuation of that promise. A promise to my grandmother. A promise to the people I've served since fourteen. A promise to the leaders who want to do better. A promise to families praying for support. A promise to elders who deserve to stay in their homes. A promise to disabled adults whose lives have been limited by systems instead of elevated by them. A promise to the future.

A future where technology doesn't overshadow people, it uplifts them. A future where innovation doesn't leave communities behind, it brings them forward. A future where independence isn't a privilege, it's standard practice. A future where dignity isn't negotiable, it's non-negotiable. A future where freedom is not a gift, it's a guarantee.

OPENING CHAPTER: PART III

THE SHIFT FROM POSSIBILITY TO PURPOSE

I returned to work the next day the same way I always did, clipboard in hand, purpose in my chest, and the same fire I had carried since fourteen. But I wasn't the same. Something had changed in how I saw people. Something had changed in how I saw the system. Something had changed in how I saw the future.

Because once you witness what technology could do, you can't pretend you didn't see it. Once you witness freedom inside a system built on control, you can't go back to "business as usual." Once you see that a simple tool, something that didn't require permission, funding, or a committee meeting, could expand someone's independence, your mind doesn't fit inside the old models anymore.

I started walking into homes, programs, and provider settings with new eyes. It wasn't just asking what supports does this person need, what are the risks, what are the goals, what are the limitations, what does the plan say. No. My questions shifted. They became: **"What's possible here? What's missing? What would freedom look like? What would independence feel like? What tools can we bring in that the system is too scared to imagine?"**

I had always been an advocate for dignity, choice, and person-centered care. That was in me long before I had language for it. It was baked into me by my grandmother, my family, my culture, my faith. But now I had a new lens. **Care doesn't have to be traditional to be effective. And support doesn't have to be intrusive to be safe.**

It was a paradigm shift that opened the door to a future that most people in the field weren't ready to talk about yet.

And this is the truth that sits at the heart of this book:

The care system is not broken because people don't care. It's broken because people don't know what's possible.

We have built entire systems around crisis, compliance, surveillance, scarcity, fear of liability, fear of change, fear of innovation, fear of "what if." But almost no one has built systems around liberation, cultural understanding, identity, dignity, choice, independence, empowerment, joy, possibility.

When I talk about tech equity, I'm not talking about gadgets. I'm talking about **the mindset shift** required to create a future where every person, disabled, aging, marginalized, overlooked, underestimated, gets to live a life with options.

Technology is not the savior. People are the savior. Technology is the tool.

My grandmother didn't need technology. She needed sovereignty. She needed safety without sacrifice, independence without isolation, support without shame. She needed continuity, connection, and dignity. And isn't that what we all want?

When we strip away the labels, disability, aging, eldercare, supportive housing, human services, healthcare, what remains are humans who want to live with choices, autonomy, respect, identity, belonging, safety, connection, and meaning.

And if technology can help sustain that

if it can make independence safer,

family connections stronger,

care more dignified,

providers more effective,

and people more empowered

then how could we not use it?

How could we not fight for it?

Did you hear what I said?!

And if technology can help sustain that, if it can make independence safer, family connections stronger, care more dignified, providers more effective, and people more empowered, then how could we not use it? How could we not fight for it? How could we not challenge a system that still sees innovation as a risk instead of a resource?

That challenge, that personal, spiritual, professional challenge, is why this book exists.

Because the truth is: **We are entering a new era of care.** One where technology isn't optional. It's inevitable. And it's time we shape that future with humanity at the center.

This book is my contribution to that future. It is a blueprint for families feeling overwhelmed, providers feeling stuck, leaders feeling pressured, innovators looking for direction, policymakers looking for clarity, communities looking for equity, elders looking for dignity, and younger generations preparing for their future.

But it is also a message for every person who has ever felt boxed in, restricted, underestimated, unheard, overlooked, dismissed, or caged by systems not built for them.

Because when my grandmother asked for her freedom, she wasn't speaking only for herself. She was speaking for generations. And my purpose, my role in this era, is to echo her voice into the future: **"Let them live with options. Let them live with dignity. Let them live with choice. Let them live free."**

This is not another tech book. This is a call to remember our humanity while building a future worthy of it.

And now that you know where this story begins, we can step into the next chapter together, not as observers, but as creators of the new normal.

CHAPTER 1: THE NEW NORMAL OF CARE

SECTION I: The System We Inherited

Let me tell you something that the field doesn't say out loud enough:

Our entire care system is built on regulations older than most of the people working in it.

And I'm not exaggerating. I'm not being dramatic. I'm stating a fact that should make every leader in this industry pause and ask themselves what we're really doing here.

Let's talk about the backbone of disability services for a moment. The ICF/MR regulations, now called ICF/IID. The original rule was written in 1988. Not updated in 1988. Not revised in 1988. *Written* in 1988. That's the foundation. That's the framework we're still operating under.

Now, since then, we've had what they call "interpretive guidelines." Little tweaks here and there. The most recent consolidated update was March 26, 2021. Before that, August 2019. Before that, February 2015. But here's what you need to understand: those were revisions, not rebuilds. They were patches on an old system, not a reimagining of what care could look like.

The core framework? Still 1988.

I don't know about anybody else, but I don't have anything from 1988 still operating in my life today. I'm lying. I might still have my beeper somewhere, but I think that was the 90s. And even then, it's collecting dust in a drawer, not running my daily operations.

But this is what we're expecting people to live by? This is the system we're calling "modern"? This is the structure that's supposed to support millions of aging adults and people with disabilities in 2025?

We've been following, and I mean really following, like it's gospel, a system from 1988. I can't even imagine still operating with the same construct for my own life. Think about it. In 1988, I didn't even meet my husband yet, and we've been together 32 years. The world has completely transformed since then. Technology has transformed. Expectations have transformed. The people we support have transformed. But the system that's supposed to serve them? It stayed still.

Let me make it plain, because I need you to really see this:

It's like trying to retrofit Mercedes-Benz EQS technology into a 1950 Chevy.

Now, when it's all finished, it might look cool. You might stand back and say, "Well, we made it work." But here's the truth. It's not doable for the average person. It's not functional for the average person. And you wind up spending more time, more money, more energy, and more frustration trying to fit modern technology into a frame that was never built for it.

A 1950 Chevy wasn't designed for Mercedes-Benz EQS systems. The frame is wrong. The infrastructure is wrong. The whole foundation is wrong. You can keep patching, keep adapting, keep adding exceptions and workarounds. And you'll keep wondering why it doesn't work the way it should.

That's exactly what we've been doing with the care system.

The 1988 framework wasn't built for aging in place. It wasn't built for remote supports or enabling technology or smart home integration. It wasn't built for digital health monitoring or the Gen X caregivers who are now running agencies. It wasn't built for the cultural diversity of the people we serve today, or for tech-enabled independence, or for the workforce crisis we're drowning in right now. It wasn't built for the massive wave of aging adults who need support, or for the new expectations of autonomy that younger generations are demanding, or for humanity-centered services that put the person, not the compliance checklist, at the center.

The system we inherited was built for a different time, a different mindset, and a different understanding of what care even means. It was built when institutions were still closing, when "technology" meant pagers and landlines, when "independence" was measured by whether someone could complete a task, not whether they had real choices about how to live their life.

Today, we are trying to squeeze modern expectations, modern lives, modern identities, and modern possibilities into a structure that was written before the internet even existed.

And here's the thing. That system worked for its time. It answered the needs of the era. It was a big step forward from institutionalization, and we should honor that. But the world has evolved. People have evolved. Needs have evolved. Technology has evolved. Expectations have evolved.

And the system?

It stayed still.

That's the inheritance we're working with. That's the "normal" we've accepted for too long. And that's exactly what has to change.

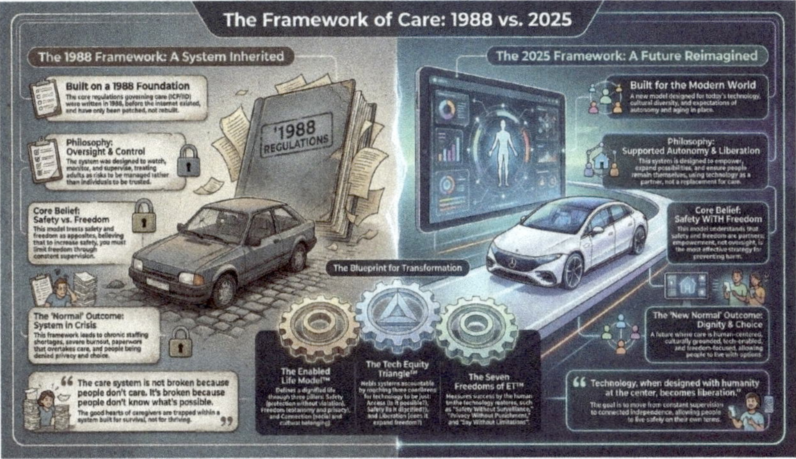

The Framework of Care: 1988 vs. 2025 — From Oversight & Control to Supported Autonomy & Liberation

SECTION II: What "Normal" Has Become

We talk a lot about "the system" as if it's this fixed, infallible structure. Something that exists beyond human decision-making, beyond culture, beyond accountability, beyond time. Like it just *is*, and we have no choice but to work within it.

But here's what we forget: systems age just like people do. They get worn. They get rigid. They become fragile in their foundation, unable to stretch or adapt to new realities. And our care system? It has aged without evolving. It got older, but it didn't get wiser. It accumulated more rules, but it didn't gain more flexibility. It added more paperwork, but it didn't add more humanity.

The Policy Context

Now, let me give you some context, because I want you to understand how we got here.

The shift away from institutions started decades ago. It was accelerated by the HCBS Waiver, cemented by the Olmstead Supreme Court decision, and strengthened by community integration mandates. These were important movements. They changed WHERE people lived. They got people out of institutions and into communities, and that mattered.

But here's what those movements didn't change: HOW we supported people once they got there.

HCBS, Home and Community-Based Services, was supposed to revolutionize community living. And in some ways, it did. But the structure, the philosophy, and the tools we used? They remained rooted in institutional thinking. We closed the buildings, yes. We moved people into homes and apartments and community settings. But the mindset? We carried it with us. We brought the institution INTO the community instead of truly leaving it behind.

And as the world moved into a digital era, as technology transformed every other industry, every other aspect of daily life, our systems didn't move with it. The rest of the world was innovating, and we were still following a 1988 playbook.

What "Normal" Looks Like Today

If you want to know what "normal" feels like in this field right now, don't ask the policymakers. Don't ask the consultants. Ask the people living it every single day.

Ask the provider CEO who can't fill shifts no matter how many job postings they put up. Ask the family member who has been on a waiting list for three years and still doesn't have services for their loved one. Ask the adult with a disability who just wants some privacy, some choice, some control over their own life, and keeps being told that's "not how the system works." Ask the aging parent who wants to stay in their home but has no safe plan to make that happen. Ask the DSP who loves this work with their whole heart but is so burned out they're not sure how much longer they can keep going.

Ask them what "normal" feels like, and you'll hear the same themes over and over:

Chronic staffing shortages that never seem to get better. Burnout so severe it becomes invisible. People just accept exhaustion as part of the job. Paperwork that grows faster than progress, where staff spend more time documenting care than actually providing it. Families begging for support that doesn't exist in their area, or doesn't exist in their budget, or just plain doesn't exist. Providers stuck in compliance mode instead of care mode, more focused on avoiding citations than creating solutions. Clinicians trying to keep people safe using outdated tools and outdated thinking. Leadership teams running on fumes while holding entire communities together through sheer willpower. And young people with disabilities demanding independence that the system simply isn't designed to support.

That's the "normal" we've created.

And here's what I need you to understand: none of this is because people don't care.

I have been in this field for 38 years, and I have never, not once, met a DSP, a clinician, a nurse, or a provider who didn't genuinely want to see the people they serve thrive. The caring is there. The hearts are there. The dedication is there.

But the system those good people inherited? It wasn't built for thriving. It was built for surviving. It was built for managing risk, not for expanding possibility. It was built for compliance, not for liberation. And no matter how much heart you bring to a broken system, the system will eventually break you if it doesn't change.

Where Policy Fails, People Pay

Here's a truth that doesn't get said enough: when regulations move slowly, people's lives move forward without them.

The policy might be stuck in 1988, but the grandmother who needs support is aging in 2025. The young man with autism who wants his own apartment isn't going to wait for the waiver to catch up to his dreams. The family trying to keep their loved one safe can't pause their lives until the state updates its interpretive guidelines.

Life doesn't wait for policy. And when there's a gap between what the regulations allow and what people actually need, everybody feels it.

Families feel the gap. They feel it in the exhaustion of being the unpaid, untrained, unsupported safety net for someone they love.

Staff feel the gap. They feel it in the impossible expectations placed on them, in the low wages that don't match the high stakes of the work they do, in the burnout that nobody seems to be addressing.

People supported feel the gap. They feel it in the lack of options, the lack of privacy, the lack of control over their own lives.

Communities of color definitely feel the gap. Because when systems are already inequitable, gaps hit hardest where resources are already thin.

Rural communities feel the gap. Urban communities feel the gap in a different way. And leaders feel the pressure to fill a hole with tools that don't exist yet, with funding that isn't there, with staff they can't find.

The Workforce Crisis

Let me talk about the workforce for a moment, because this is where the cracks become canyons.

DSPs and caregivers are exhausted. And I don't mean regular tired. I mean bone-deep, soul-weary exhaustion that comes from years of being asked to do more with less. They're underpaid for work that requires immense skill, patience, and emotional labor. They're overcommitted because there's no one to cover the shifts that need covering. They're oversupervised in all the wrong ways. Paperwork, check-ins, compliance monitoring. And undersupported in all the right ways. Nobody's asking them what THEY need to do this work sustainably. Nobody's investing in their growth, their wellness, their futures.

They love this work. I've seen it. They love the people they support. They show up with their whole hearts, day after day, even when the system makes it nearly impossible to do the job well.

But love is not enough when the structure itself is unsustainable. You can't love your way out of a 60% turnover rate. You can't heart-emoji your way through a staffing shortage that's been building for decades. At some point, we have to look at the system and admit: this isn't working. And the people paying the highest price are the ones with the least power to change it.

The Generational Reality

And then we add this truth to everything I just said:

Gen X is aging. I'm Gen X. I'm thinking about my own future now, about what care will look like when I need it.

Baby Boomers are aging. The largest generation in American history is entering the phase of life where support becomes essential.

Millennials are aging too. Time doesn't stop for any of us.

And here's something the field doesn't always acknowledge: people with disabilities are living longer than ever before. That's a victory. A result of better healthcare, better supports, better advocacy. But it also means the system needs to support people across longer lifespans, with changing needs, with different expectations than previous generations had.

The largest wave of aging adults in U.S. history is happening right now. Not ten years from now. Not "eventually." RIGHT NOW.

And we have more people needing support than ever before, while simultaneously having fewer people available to provide that support. The math doesn't work. The model doesn't work. Something has to give.

What People Actually Want

Meanwhile, in the middle of all this crisis, the people at the center of our services are asking for something pretty simple.

They want independence. Real independence, not independence that comes with a staff person hovering in the corner.

They want privacy. The ability to close a door, to have a moment alone, to not be watched every second of the day.

They want choice. Real choices about how they live, where they live, who supports them, how they spend their time.

They want cultural competency. Services and supports that understand and respect who they are, where they come from, what matters to them.

They want connection. To family, to community, to the world, to relationships that matter.

They want tools that match the pace of their life. Not tools designed in

1988 for problems that existed in 1988.

And above all, they want dignity. They want to be treated like the full human beings they are.

People want freedom WITH safety. They want autonomy WITH support. They want care WITHOUT losing themselves in the process.

Is that really too much to ask?

But old systems can't deliver modern needs. You can't get 2025 outcomes from a 1988 framework. The gap between what people need and what the system offers is widening every single day. And widening gaps don't just stay gaps. They become crises.

The Bottom Line

This is the "new normal" we're living in. A normal we didn't choose, but one we must address.

And here is the part that should make every leader in this field pause:

The people we support have changed. They're living longer, expecting more, demanding dignity that previous generations weren't allowed to ask for.

The world around us has changed. Technology has transformed every other industry, every other aspect of life.

But the system designed to support them? It hasn't changed. Not really. Not at the foundation.

That's the gap this book is about closing.

SECTION III: The Three Truths of Future Care

There comes a point in every field where the old story no longer fits the reality of people's lives. Where the assumptions we've been operating under for decades finally collide with a world that has moved on without us.

We are living in that moment right now.

The care system has spent decades trying to solve modern challenges with outdated assumptions, outdated models, and outdated fears. We keep applying 1988 thinking to 2025 problems and wondering why nothing gets better. But the future won't wait for us to get comfortable.

It won't pause while we debate whether change is necessary. The future is already here. It's just waiting for us to catch up.

If we're going to redesign care for the next generation, we have to start by grounding ourselves in three truths. Not trends that might fade. Not theories that sound good in a conference room. Not opinions that change depending on who's in the room. I'm talking about truths. The kind of reality that will shape everything we build next, whether we acknowledge it or not.

Any system, leader, policymaker, provider, family, or innovator who ignores these truths will get left behind. Not because I say so, but because reality has a way of catching up with all of us eventually.

So let me lay them out for you.

TRUTH #1: People Want Independence More Than They Want Oversight

Here's something that unites every generation. Gen X, Millennials, Boomers, Gen Z, and everyone coming after us. We all want the same thing at our core:

Independence.

Not isolation. Not abandonment. Not "figure it out on your own." Independence. The ability to make our own decisions, to live on our own terms, to have privacy and autonomy and dignity and choice. To have space. To be trusted. To have control over our own lives.

You hear it everywhere if you listen. People say, "I want to stay in my home as long as possible." They say, "I want to make my own decisions." They say, "I don't want someone standing over me." They say, "I don't want to feel watched." They say, "I don't want to be treated like a child just because I need some help."

And when you ask people with disabilities what they want, really ask them, and really listen, the core answer is the same: "Respect my independence."

This isn't complicated. It's human.

But here's the problem: the system was built on oversight, not independence. It was designed to watch, to correct, to monitor, to supervise, to check-in, to "manage." The whole philosophy was built around making sure nothing goes wrong. Which sounds good until you realize that in practice, it means treating adults like they can't be trusted to live their own lives.

And here's what I've learned after 38 years in this field: independence doesn't grow under surveillance. It doesn't flourish when someone is always watching, always correcting, always hovering. Independence grows under support, under trust, and with the right tools.

When we design systems for control, people shrink. I've seen it happen. They become smaller versions of themselves because the system doesn't leave room for them to be anything else.

But when we design systems for freedom? People rise. They surprise us. They exceed every limitation we thought they had. Because most of those limitations were never theirs to begin with. They were the system's limitations, projected onto the people we serve.

This is why enabling technology matters so much to me.

Enabling technology moves us from constant supervision to connected independence. It lets people live safely, on their own terms, without someone always in their space, while still being supported when they need it. That's the balance people are asking for. That's what freedom with safety actually looks like.

Independence is not a luxury for people who "earn it." It's a human need. And the future of care must honor that, or it will fail the very people it claims to serve.

TRUTH #2: Technology Can Support What the Workforce Can No Longer Sustain

Let me say the quiet part out loud, because somebody needs to:

We do not have enough staff to support people in the traditional way. Not now. Not next year. Not ten years from now.

This is not a temporary problem. It's not a blip caused by the pandemic that will correct itself. The workforce crisis is structural. It's baked into the foundation of how we've built this system.

Think about what we're dealing with: low pay for work that requires immense skill and emotional labor. High burnout because the expectations are impossible. High turnover because people can only run on fumes for so long before they leave. An aging workforce with fewer young people entering the field to replace them. Increased demand as the population ages and people with disabilities live longer. And on top of all that, increased expectations for independence and more medically complex needs that require specialized knowledge.

We are asking human beings to carry the weight of an entire system on their backs, and then blaming them when the system cracks.

And here's what I think about often, what I hear when I sit in ISP meetings and around planning tables: people never question the wrong in our system. They never ask, "Would this be acceptable in another industry? Would this be acceptable in a similar industry with higher standards?"

Let me tell you what I mean.

Some people know, they KNOW, that the staff have been on shift for 24 hours straight. Sometimes even three days straight. We have had some serious staffing issues, and people just accept it because at least there's "coverage." But we know for a fact that the human body cannot sustain that level of work and deliver quality care. It's not possible. The body isn't designed for it.

But what is the system more concerned with? Do you have a body there? That's it. It doesn't matter if that body is actually able to do anything. It doesn't matter if that staff person is so exhausted they can barely function. The question is just: is someone physically present?

And a staff person who has been working for 24 or 48 hours is not keen. They're doing their best. I want to be clear about that. They are doing their absolute best. But at some point, the body says it's time to go to sleep. The body says, "Okay, we have to shut down for a little bit." Their eyes may be open, but their mind has completely shut down.

What benefit does that give to the person with a disability who is waiting for a service to be provided? What benefit does it give when someone needs a question answered, or needs assistance, and the staff person is physically present but mentally gone? What are we actually providing at that point?

But see, when you have technology in place, with all the proper systems, backup batteries, and safeguards, technology doesn't get tired the same way a human body does. Technology doesn't need to sleep after a 24-hour shift. Technology maintains the same level of alertness at hour one as it does at hour forty.

And here's something else I always think about: hospitals.

Hospitals are handling the most serious of situations. Acute care. Life and death. And yet, if you think about it, they actually provide less direct support in terms of bodies standing over your shoulder. When you're in the most serious medical situation of your life, there is not a nurse hovering in the corner of your room watching you breathe. There is not a CNA standing at the foot of your bed staring at you around the clock. In the most acute care situations, the situations where the stakes are literally life and death, there is no one standing over your shoulder.

Why? Because they have technology. They have monitors. They have systems. They have alerts.

Now, I understand hospitals are reimbursed at higher rates than any ICF or HCBS waiver service. But that's not my point. My point is this: if technology-supported care is acceptable in the most serious, life-or-death situations, if it's good enough for the ICU, good enough for post-surgical care, good enough for acute medical crises, why is it not acceptable for everyday life in the community?

Why are community-based services MORE rigid than the intensive care unit?

Think about that. A hospital can monitor someone recovering from open-heart surgery using technology, and that's considered excellent care. But a person with a disability living in their own home, who is NOT in a medical crisis, needs a staff person physically present around the clock or it's considered unsafe?

The logic doesn't hold.

And here's what makes it even more absurd: hospitals are now exploring "Hospital at Home" programs. They're moving toward MORE flexibility, allowing people to recover in their own homes with remote monitoring and technology-supported care. The acute care system is evolving, expanding what's possible, embracing technology as a partner.

Meanwhile, we're over here in community-based services still trying to jack up that 1988 Ford Escort with 450,000 miles on it, insisting that the only way to provide "real" care is to have a human body standing in the room at all times.

The hospital system is moving forward. Why are we standing still?

I've done this work for a long time now, and I can tell you from experience: technology gives you MORE support, not less. It gives you more data, more accurate data. I'm no longer guessing if someone had a good night's sleep. I now know for sure because the technology captured the data points. I can take that information and provide it to the right clinician, the right team, and we can look at it through a lens that leads to much more meaningful care.

Technology can monitor safely without requiring a staff person to sit in someone's living room for eight hours. It can alert immediately when something is wrong. It can remind automatically so staff aren't playing medication police all day. It can reduce paperwork. And Lord knows we need less paperwork in this field. It can analyze patterns that human beings would never catch because we're too busy putting out fires. It can predict risks before they become crises. It can extend staff bandwidth so the people we do have can focus on the work that actually requires human connection.

And here's what happens when staff feel supported, when they have tools that make their jobs doable, when they feel respected and empowered instead of overwhelmed and abandoned: retention goes up. Burnout goes down. Quality of care improves. Staff actually want to stay in the field because the work becomes meaningful again instead of just exhausting.

Even doctors benefit. When a clinician can receive real data about what's happening with a person who is non-verbal or who can't articulate what's going on, not just "the staff thinks he seemed off today" but actual patterns and trends, they can make real treatment decisions. They become more engaged because they're not just guessing. They probably want to serve more people with disabilities because they feel like they can actually practice medicine, not just make educated guesses.

We're not just guessing anymore. We're using quality data to guide our judgment. That's what modern care looks like.

The future of care isn't about choosing between technology and people. That's a false choice. It's about using technology to support people. The people we serve AND the people who serve them. The workforce crisis is a human crisis, and technology is one of the most powerful tools we have to address it.

TRUTH #3: Safety and Freedom Are Not Opposites, They Are Partners

For decades, our field has talked about safety and freedom like they're enemies. Like choosing one automatically means sacrificing the other. Like you have to pick a side.

The old belief went like this: More freedom equals more risk. More supervision equals more safety. So if you want people to be safe, you have to limit their freedom. You have to watch them. You have to control the environment. You have to manage every variable.

But that was always a false choice. And I think deep down, most people in this field know it.

People do not become safer when we take away their independence. They don't become safer when we strip away their choices, their privacy, their autonomy. In fact, the opposite often happens. People who feel controlled, who feel watched, who feel like they have no agency over their own lives, they disengage. They stop trying. They become smaller. And that creates its own kind of danger.

People become safer when we support their independence intelligently. When we give them tools. When we trust them. When we design environments that protect without suffocating.

Safety and freedom are not competing values. They are complementary values. They need each other.

Here's a truth that people in this field don't want to admit: oversight doesn't prevent harm. Empowerment does.

Think about it. When people understand their options, when they have tools that support them, when they feel respected, when they feel culturally seen, when they feel connected to others, when they feel trusted, when they feel prepared, they make better decisions. They take better care of themselves. They ask for help when they need it because they're not afraid of losing their freedom if they admit they're struggling.

But when people are stripped of agency? When they feel like asking for help means losing control of their lives? That's when harm increases. That's when people hide problems until they become crises. That's when the system fails the very people it's supposed to protect.

Technology, when designed with humanity and culture in mind, becomes the bridge between safety and freedom. Sensors don't control people. They protect them. Smart supports don't limit independence. They expand it. Dashboards don't eliminate risk. They help us understand it before it becomes a crisis.

Freedom is not the opposite of safety. Freedom is the partner of safety. Freedom is the STRATEGY of safety.

If we don't get this right, if we keep treating safety and freedom as enemies, the future will leave us behind. Because the people we serve are already demanding both. And they're right to demand it.

The Ground Beneath the Future

These three truths are not predictions about what might happen someday. They are the ground we're already standing on. They are the foundation of everything coming next.

The world is changing whether we're ready or not. People are demanding more. Technology is advancing faster than our policies can keep up. Families want better options. Staff want better support. Communities want culturally relevant care. Aging adults want dignity. Adults with disabilities want freedom.

And the system has a choice: evolve, or become irrelevant.

This book is about evolution. It's about building a care model that honors humanity, dignity, culture, and possibility. It's about stepping boldly into the new normal and shaping it. Not waiting for it to happen to us, but building the future we actually want to live in.

That's what these truths are for. They're the foundation. Now let's build on them.

SECTION IV: The Cultural Gap in Modern Care

Why tech equity is about people, not products.

If there's one thing the disability and aging fields need to understand, and

I mean really understand, not just nod at in a training session, it's this:

Technology cannot be equitable if care has never been equitable.

We like to talk about innovation as if it's neutral. As if technology is this magical force that will solve all our problems if we just "adopt" it. As if buying devices automatically creates access, inclusion, or dignity. But that's not how any of this works.

Here's the truth: technology reflects the system it's built on. If you layer technology onto a system that has never centered culture, you don't get tech equity. You get tech gaps. You get tools that don't land in the communities that need them most. You get rejection from families who weren't consulted. You get fear from elders who don't see themselves in the solution. You get resistance from marginalized groups who have learned, through generations of experience, not to trust systems that claim to be "helping" them.

Technology does not magically fix cultural inequity. It magnifies it.

It shows us who was considered when the solution was designed, and who was ignored. It shows us who gets options and who gets restrictions. It shows us who is trusted to make their own decisions, and who is surveilled. It shows us who receives empowerment, and who receives control dressed up as "support."

This is the part of the conversation most leaders want to avoid. It's uncomfortable. It requires self-examination. It requires admitting that our systems have never been culturally grounded, and that adding technology to an inequitable foundation just creates new forms of the same old problems.

But we will not build a future of care by avoiding truth. So let me show you what I mean.

When Culture Is Ignored, Equity Fails

Let me give you some real examples of what happens when cultural understanding is missing in care, and how technology, used correctly, could shift everything.

Example 1: The Family Who Rejected Cameras

A team I worked with insisted that in-home cameras would "keep a person safe." They had done the assessment. They had the technology ready to deploy. They were confident this was the right solution.

The family said absolutely not.

And the team was confused. They kept pushing. "But it's for safety. But it's the best option. But other families use this." They couldn't understand why this family was resistant to something that seemed so obviously beneficial.

But here's what they didn't understand, and what they never bothered to ask about:

For this Black family, "being watched" had a very different historical meaning. Surveillance wasn't neutral for them. It was tied to profiling, to criminalization, to fear, to harm, to systems that had never protected them. Cameras in their home didn't feel like safety. It felt like danger. It felt like the same systems that had always watched them. Not to help, but to catch them doing something wrong.

To the team, cameras meant protection. To the family, cameras meant threat. Based on generational memory and lived reality.

Safety cannot be defined without understanding culture. Technology cannot be adopted without trust. And trust has to be earned, especially with communities that have been harmed by systems claiming to help them.

Example 2: The Elders Who Didn't Want Strangers in Their Home

I've seen this situation play out many times: elders who refuse support, and agencies that can't figure out why.

The agency sees staff as "help." They're sending trained workers into homes to provide care. What's the problem?

But the elders see strangers. People who don't look like them, don't speak their language, don't understand their traditions, don't know how to show respect in the ways their culture requires. The staff might be perfectly competent, but they feel like outsiders. And for many elders, especially those from immigrant communities, from tight-knit cultural communities, from communities with deep traditions around family and care, having an outsider in your home feels wrong. It feels unsafe in a way that has nothing to do with their professional credentials.

A culturally-aligned technology solution could have changed everything. Smart sensors that monitor safety without requiring a stranger to sit in the living room. Remote check-ins in the elder's own language. Linguistic accessibility tools that allow communication without requiring the elder to speak English. Technology that maintains safety without violating trust.

But if culture isn't part of the solution, people won't accept the solution. It's that simple.

Example 3: The Young Deaf Woman Who Was Left Out of Life

This one still sits with me.

I once supported a young Deaf woman who could do almost everything independently. She cooked her own meals. She signed fluently. She navigated the community with confidence. She advocated for herself. She was capable, intelligent, and had a full life she wanted to live.

And yet, her staff would leave her behind when they took other people on outings.

Not because she couldn't go. Not because she didn't want to go. But because they didn't understand her culture.

They would say things like, "She won't enjoy the nightclub." "She can't hear the music." "It's too loud for her." "It'll be too hard to communicate."

But what they didn't understand, what they never bothered to learn, was this: Deaf people experience music. They experience vibration. They experience rhythm. They experience the bass in their chest, the movement of bodies around them, the energy of a room, the community and culture of being out in the world.

She didn't need someone to help her "hear." She needed someone to help her belong.

And because staff didn't understand Deaf culture, because they made assumptions based on their own hearing-centered view of the world, she missed out on life. Over and over again, she was left behind while others went out and had experiences she was fully capable of having.

A few simple supports could have changed her entire experience. Communication apps. Video relay tools. Captioning technology. Vibrating alert devices. And most importantly, staff who were trained to understand Deaf culture instead of making assumptions about what Deaf people can and cannot enjoy.

When we finally corrected the issue, when we got her the right support and she went dancing with staff who understood, she lit up from the inside out. I watched it happen.

And she said something to me that changed the way I see everything:

"I always wanted this. Y'all just assumed I didn't."

That one sentence. That's the whole problem with our field in one sentence.

Her disability wasn't the barrier. The system's imagination was.

Culture Shapes Technology Adoption

When culture is ignored, technology becomes intrusive. It becomes misused, misunderstood, rejected, feared. It gets stripped of its purpose and becomes just another tool that doesn't work for the people it was supposed to help.

But when culture is centered? Technology becomes liberating. It becomes empowering, accessible, trusted, wanted. It becomes life-changing.

Here's what I need leaders to understand: technology doesn't build trust. People build trust. Culture builds trust. And trust is the foundation of adoption. You can have the most advanced, most effective technology in the world, and if people don't trust it, if they don't see themselves in it, if it wasn't designed with them in mind, they won't use it.

Cultural Competency IS Tech Competency

We cannot build tech equity without cultural humility. Without representation in who designs solutions and who implements them. Without community voice at the table from the beginning, not just at the end when you're trying to figure out why your solution didn't work. Without historical awareness of why certain communities are suspicious of certain technologies. Without trauma-informed leadership that understands how systems have harmed people in the past. Without linguistic accessibility that doesn't treat English as the default. Without intersectional understanding that recognizes people hold multiple identities at once. Without cross-cultural communication skills. Without deep respect for identity. Without co-creation WITH the communities we serve, not just creation FOR them.

Because technology that is not culturally grounded will always feel like a threat, a burden, or an imposition to someone. But technology that respects culture feels like support, like freedom, like empowerment.

This is why you cannot talk about enabling technology without talking about cultural equity. They are not separate conversations. They are the same conversation.

This is why this book exists. To weave together the conversations that the field has kept separate for too long.

Because the truth is simple:

There is no tech equity without cultural equity.

There is no innovation without humanity.

There is no future without inclusion.

SECTION V: A New Era of Care: Why We Can't Go Back

There are moments in history when the old way becomes impossible to sustain. Moments when circumstances collide with courage. When systems meet reality. When communities meet truth. When leaders must decide whether they will adapt or collapse.

We are living in one of those moments right now.

The world around us has shifted. The needs of people have evolved. The expectations of independence have grown in ways the original system designers never anticipated. The demographics have changed dramatically. The pressure on staff is greater than it has ever been. And the tools at our fingertips are more advanced than anything this field has ever seen.

And yet, we keep trying to run 2025 lives on a 1988 system.

We keep trying to solve staffing shortages with the same hiring strategies from thirty years ago. We keep trying to address burnout by asking staff to just push through. We keep trying to meet aging needs with models designed for a younger population. We keep talking about disability rights while operating systems that limit freedom. We keep acknowledging cultural inequities while implementing culturally blind solutions. We keep responding to safety concerns with more surveillance instead of smarter support. We keep managing crisis after crisis instead of building systems that prevent them. We keep trying to heal institutional trauma while recreating institutional dynamics in community settings. We keep watching families drown in overwhelm while offering them the same inadequate options.

And we keep doing all of this with strategies that were created before the internet even existed.

Here is the truth we cannot ignore anymore:

We cannot improve the system by repeating it. We cannot transform care by preserving what harms us. We cannot move forward by holding onto what was never built for us in the first place.

The traditional model of care cannot carry us into the future. The math doesn't work. The workforce capacity doesn't exist. The expectations of autonomy won't shrink just because we're not ready to meet them. The population of aging adults won't decrease just because we haven't figured out how to serve them. The need for safe, dignified, culturally grounded support won't fade just because it's hard to provide.

We cannot go back. Going back is not an option for the people we serve. It was never really an option at all.

What Must Change

Homes must become smarter. Not because technology is trendy, but because smart homes allow people to live safely with less intrusion, more privacy, and more dignity.

Systems must become stronger. Not stronger in the sense of more rigid or more controlling, but stronger in the sense of more responsive, more adaptive, more capable of meeting people where they actually are.

Practices must become more culturally responsive. Not as an add-on or an afterthought, but as a foundation. Culture cannot be something we address in a training once a year. It has to be woven into everything we do.

Leadership must become more adaptive. The leaders who will thrive in the next era of care are not the ones who have all the answers. They're the ones who are willing to ask better questions, to listen deeply, to change course when the evidence demands it.

Technology must become more equitable. Not technology for technology's sake, but technology designed with the communities it serves, technology that expands freedom instead of restricting it, technology that respects culture and builds trust.

Care must reflect the lives people want to live. Not the limitations we are afraid to release. Not the fears that have governed our field for decades. The actual lives that actual people want to live.

Building Requires Courage

This next era of care is not one we ease into. It's one we build into. And building requires courage.

Courage requires imagination. It requires the willingness to look at what we've always done and say, "This isn't working anymore." It requires leaders who can hold the discomfort of not knowing exactly what comes next while still moving forward.

And imagination requires leaders willing to say out loud, "We can do better than this."

We cannot cling to "how we've always done it" when how we've always done it is failing people. We cannot hide behind outdated regulations when those regulations were written for a different world. We cannot keep calling surveillance "safety" when the people being watched don't feel safe at all. We cannot prioritize compliance over care, paperwork over people, fear over possibility.

We cannot keep underestimating adults with disabilities. They know what they want. They know what they need. They are waiting for us to catch up to what they've been telling us for years.

We cannot keep undervaluing elders. They have wisdom. They have preferences. They have the right to age with dignity, in their own homes, on their own terms.

We cannot keep overburdening staff while underpaying them and then wondering why they leave. We cannot keep underutilizing technology while complaining that we don't have enough workers.

We owe people more than that.

We owe staff relief. Real relief. Not pizza parties and thank you cards, but sustainable workloads, fair pay, and tools that make impossible jobs possible.

We owe families peace. Not the exhausted peace of giving up, but the real peace that comes from knowing their loved ones are safe, supported, and thriving.

We owe communities equity. Not lip service to diversity, but actual investment in culturally grounded care that reaches everyone.

We owe elders dignity. The dignity of choice, of privacy, of being seen as whole people with full lives, not just bodies to be managed.

We owe adults with disabilities liberation. Not just community placement, but actual freedom. The freedom to take risks, make mistakes, grow, change, and live.

We owe future generations a system worthy of them. Because the children being born today will grow up to need these services, or to work in them, or to have family members who depend on them. What kind of system do we want to leave them?

The New Reality

The future of care must be human-centered, putting people at the heart of every decision. It must be culturally grounded, built on respect for the diverse communities we serve. It must be tech-enabled, using the tools of our time to expand what's possible. It must be freedom-focused, prioritizing independence and choice over control and restriction. It must be equity-led, ensuring that the benefits of innovation reach everyone, not just those with resources. And it must be innovation-driven, willing to try new approaches even when the old ways feel safer.

This is not a trend. This is not a pilot program. This is not a "new initiative" that will fade when the funding runs out. This is not a suggestion.

This is the new reality.

And the leaders who fail to embrace it, who cling to outdated models, who ignore technological evolution, who dismiss cultural intelligence, who fear innovation more than they fear stagnation, will not survive the next decade of care. I don't say that to be harsh. I say it because it's true. The world is moving, and leaders who refuse to move with it will find themselves running organizations that no one wants to work for and no one wants to receive services from.

This Is Our Moment

We are entering a new era. An era where independence is the expectation, not the exception. Where dignity is non-negotiable. Where freedom is the priority, not the reward for good behavior. Where technology is the support that makes freedom possible. Where people remain at the center of every decision, every policy, every practice. Where culture is respected and woven into everything we do. Where equity is the measure of our success, not just our intention. Where safety is integrated into life, not imposed on it. Where staff are empowered to do meaningful work. Where communities are heard and included. Where systems are rebuilt from the ground up to serve the people they were always supposed to serve.

This book is the blueprint for that future.

Not just for leaders, though leaders need to read it. Not just for families, though families will find themselves in these pages. Not just for tech innovators, though innovators will find guidance here. Not just for policymakers, though policy must change for any of this to work.

This book is for every person who believes the future of care can be better than its past. And who is ready to be part of creating it.

This is our moment. This is our shift. This is our call.

We cannot go back. We won't go back.

The only direction is forward.

CHAPTER 2: UNDERSTANDING ENABLING TECHNOLOGY LIKE A HUMAN, NOT A DEVICE

SECTION I: Introduction: The Enabling Technology Ecosystem

We often treat technology like it's a solution in itself. As if buying a device can solve loneliness. As if installing a sensor can fix culture. As if a dashboard can replace understanding. We act like technology is magic, like it will automatically transform care just because it exists.

But here is the part the industry overlooks every single time:

Technology doesn't transform care. People transform care. Technology just supports the transformation.

The problem has never been technology itself. The problem is how systems have used it. They've used technology to watch people, not to support them. To control, not to liberate. To address compliance requirements, not to honor humanity. To reduce staffing costs, not to strengthen independence. To manage liability, not to expand autonomy. To gather data for reports, not to build dignity in daily life.

And people notice. They always notice.

This is why people hesitate when you introduce technology into their lives. It's not because they lack "tech literacy." It's because they have system literacy. They know what institutions feel like. They know what "monitoring" has meant historically for people who look like them, people in their situation, people who have been controlled by systems that claimed to be helping. They know the difference between something that is actually for their benefit and something that is for the convenience of the system.

No adult with a disability needs a policy degree to understand when a device is being used to restrict their freedom instead of expanding it.

They feel it. No aging adult needs a tech tutorial to understand when a tool is being introduced without any regard for their culture, their voice, or their comfort. They know. And no family needs a training manual to recognize when something is not aligned with the dignity they want for their loved one. They can tell.

The truth is simple, and I need you to really hear this:

People don't fear technology. They fear losing themselves.

So how do we use technology in a way that doesn't make people smaller? How do we build something that actually serves the person? That's what this chapter is about. And to get there, I need to teach you how I think about technology, because I've essentially created my own language for it.

Assistive Technology: One Device, One Need

Most people understand assistive technology. It's a piece of technology that addresses a very specific function or a very specific need. It works in a one-to-one ratio. Someone needs help remembering to wake up at a certain time? That's an alarm clock. Most of us have that assistive technology in our lives already. For a person with a cognitive disability or for a senior, it might be something a little more advanced, but the concept is the same. One device. One need. One solution.

And there's nothing wrong with that. Assistive technology is important. It comes after we've assessed the person's needs, their dreams, their wishes, their outcomes. It's part of what I think of as translating or innovating the person-centered planning process. You look at what the person wants for their life, and then you look for a piece of technology that can help address one of those wishes, dreams, needs, or outcomes.

But here's where I take it a step further.

Enabling Technology: Devices Working Together as a Team

If I'm trying to get to the point of remote supports, meaning somebody being supported without having 100% in-your-face direct support, without constant human presence hovering over them, then I can't just think about one device at a time. I have to think about how each piece of assistive technology can perform together as a team to provide that level of support.

This is where I go back to my hospital example, and the reason I use this is because most of us know what it means. Either we've been to a hospital, we've been a patient, or we're avid watchers of ER. Either way, we know what the situation looks like.

Think about the ICU. You have a heart monitor. You have a blood pressure monitor. You have a pulse ox monitor. Each one has a different function it's performing on the patient. But they don't work in isolation. They all come together and work together as a team. If one goes off, the next one is alerted. They support one another to collect data. Maybe the pulse ox indicates that oxygen levels are going down, and that information communicates to check that blood pressure. They're talking to each other. They're functioning as a unit.

That's enabling technology. It's not just one device. It's multiple devices working together, each performing its function, but all of them connected in a way that creates comprehensive support.

The Enabling Technology Ecosystem: How You Actually Get to Remote Supports

Now here's where I take it even further, and you won't hear a lot of people use this terminology because I essentially made it up.

Once I understand how assistive technology works, and I understand how those devices can function together in an enabling technology way, then I have to ask: how do those relate to everything else? How do they connect to human supports? How does the technology communicate with the people who need to respond?

Because here's what I see constantly in this field: people are focused on the device. They just want to get one device and think that's going to get them to remote supports. But one device can't get someone to remote supports. What gets someone to remote supports is what I call the Enabling Technology Ecosystem.

The Enabling Technology Ecosystem is the holistic approach. It's everything working together. Let me break it down:

Assessment. You start by understanding the person's needs, dreams, wishes, and outcomes. Just like any treatment plan or plan of care.

Matching. You match the person with the right technology. What devices address their specific needs? What assistive technology makes sense for their situation?

Communication structure. You build the system so that the devices can talk to a central point as much as possible. The left hand has to know what the right hand is doing. You can't just have a whole bunch of pieces of technology that don't communicate with each other. That would be overwhelming for anybody.

Human supports. You add in the human component, both direct and indirect. How does mom fit in? How does dad fit in? How does the family fit in? How does the neighbor fit in if that's relevant? How do the direct support professionals fit in? How do the clinicians, the doctors, the OT, PT, speech pathologist, the nutritionist, how do they all get the good information that the technology is collecting? The technology can't work without the human. You need that human component.

Systems requirements. You address regulations, family desires, cultural needs, personal preferences, backup systems, emergency planning. What happens if the technology fails? What are the safeguards? What are the backup plans?

Training, training, training. Everyone who touches this ecosystem needs to understand how it works. The person being supported. The family. The DSPs. The remote caregivers. The clinicians. Training is not optional.

Remote DSP or caregivers. The people who are monitoring, responding, and supporting from a distance. They're part of the ecosystem too.

When I put all of that together, I am creating an Enabling Technology Ecosystem. It's not just one device coming to address one situation. It's the entire system: the technology, the people, the supports, the data flow, the communication pathways, the backup systems, the safeguards, the training, the learning, the growth. All of it working together.

And this ecosystem is what allows or enables remote supports in a safe, functional, and innovatively fun manner.

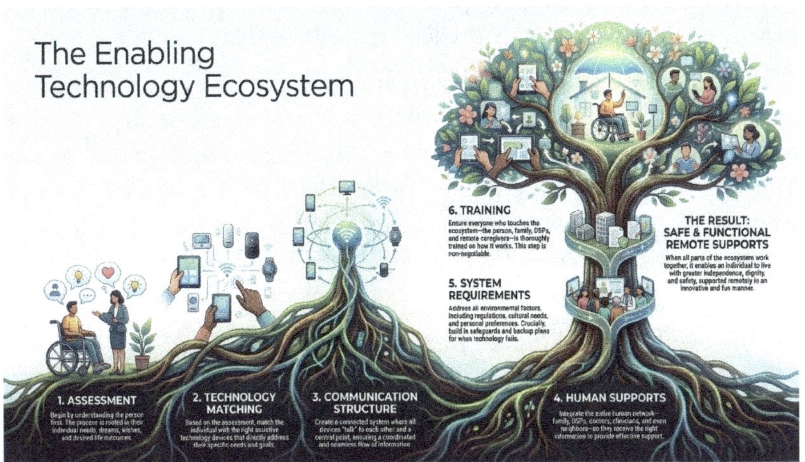

The Enabling Technology Ecosystem: The holistic approach to Remote Supports — Assessment, Technology Matching, Communication Structure, Human Supports, System Requirements, and Training

Without the ecosystem approach, you will have gaps. And those gaps are exactly what we're trying to be proactive in addressing. Most of us have tons of technology in our homes right now. And most of us have yet to figure out how they all function for our greater good. That's the gap I'm filling.

The Ritmo Framework™: The Soundtrack of a Dignified Life

I've explained the technical progression from assistive technology to enabling technology to the ecosystem. But when I'm teaching this to providers, to families, to anyone trying to understand how all of this comes together, I don't start with devices and systems. I start with music. And I start with relationships.

I call it the Ritmo Framework. Ritmo is the Spanish word for rhythm. And here's what I've learned after 38 years in this field: a dignified life requires a steady, reliable beat. Not sporadic alarms. Not random interventions. Not crisis management disguised as care. A rhythm. A flow. A soundtrack that keeps playing even when things get hard.

In this framework, technology acts as the rhythm section. It keeps the beat so the person can play the lead melody of their own life.

But here's what makes this framework different. The music isn't just a metaphor for technology. It's a metaphor for life itself. Because the way technology builds is the same way relationships build. The same way families build. The same way communities build. When I teach this framework, I teach both progressions together, because they move in rhythm with each other. That's why it's called Ritmo. It's the rhythm of life.

Let me break it down in four movements.

Movement 1: The Beat. The Individual. This is the individual device. The assistive technology. One instrument playing its part. A motion sensor. A smart speaker. A medication reminder. Each one has a function. Each one contributes something. But one instrument alone doesn't make music. It makes noise. Important noise, maybe. Helpful noise. But not yet a song. And in life, this is where we all start. As individuals. With our own gifts, our own functions, our own contributions. But we weren't meant to stay there.

Movement 2: The Groove. The Courtship. This is where the devices start talking to each other. This is enabling technology. The interoperability. The relationship between instruments. Think about a drummer and a bass player locking in together. They're not playing the same notes, but they're listening to each other. They're responding to each other. They're creating something neither could create alone. That's the groove. That's when the motion sensor tells the smart speaker to announce something. That's when the door sensor communicates with the remote monitoring platform. And in life, this is the courtship. Two individuals learning each other's language. Building trust. Figuring out how to move together. The devices are courting each other. They're learning each other's rhythms. They're building a relationship.

Movement 3: The Song. The Marriage and Family. This is the Enabling Technology Environment. The structured smart home. Now we have a composition. The instruments are playing together, and there's a structure to it. Verses and choruses. Patterns and progressions. The home itself becomes a living system that responds to the person. Lights adjust. Temperature responds. Alerts flow where they need to go. The song has been written, and it plays reliably, day after day. And in life, this is the marriage. This is the family. This is the home where everything lives together and functions as one unit. The courtship has become a commitment. The relationship has become a household. There's structure now. There's reliability. There's a song that plays every morning and every night, and everyone knows their part.

Movement 4: The Soundtrack. The Community. This is the Enabling Technology Ecosystem. The full orchestra. The village. Now we're not just talking about devices anymore. We're talking about humans. Remote support staff. Family members. Case managers. Clinicians. Backup systems. Policies that allow this to happen. Funding that sustains it. Training that keeps everyone sharp. Documentation that proves it's working. The soundtrack is what plays behind your entire life. It's not just one song. It's every song, every transition, every movement from morning to night, from Monday to Sunday, from crisis to calm. And in life, this is the community. No family survives alone. No marriage thrives in isolation. We need the village. We need the neighbors and the church and the support network and the systems that catch us when we fall. The soundtrack never stops because the community never stops. The music keeps playing. The support keeps flowing. The rhythm holds.

That's the Ritmo Framework. The Beat. The Groove. The Song. The Soundtrack. The Individual. The Courtship. The Marriage. The Community.

Two progressions moving in rhythm with each other. Because technology should mirror life. And life, when it's working right, has a rhythm to it. A flow. A soundtrack that carries you through.

When I'm assessing a person's situation, I'm listening for where they are in this progression. Do they have a beat? Do they have a groove? Do they have a song? Or are they trying to live their life in silence, with no rhythm at all, just waiting for the next crisis to interrupt them?

My job is to help them build their soundtrack. And once that soundtrack is playing, once the rhythm is steady and the music is flowing, they can finally do what they were always meant to do: live their life as the lead melody.

The Dean Martin Principle: Why Context Is Everything

Before I move to the frameworks, I need to tell you about a principle that sits underneath all of this. I call it the Dean Martin Principle, and it's the reason why generic technology will never be enough for this population.

I'll tell you the full story in Chapter 4. But here's what you need to know now.

There was a woman we supported who, when she was in distress, would say "Dean Martin." Not because she wanted to listen to Dean Martin. Not because she was confused. Because decades ago, when she was a little girl, her grandmother would calm her down by playing Dean Martin records. And somewhere in her memory, "Dean Martin" became the code for "I need help. I need comfort. I need someone to come."

Now imagine if we had programmed a generic AI assistant in her home. She says "Dean Martin," and the system starts playing Dean Martin songs or pulling up his Wikipedia page. The system heard her words. But it didn't understand her meaning.

That's the Dean Martin Principle: technology must be programmed to honor personal meaning over universal definitions.

A system that treats every user the same is not equitable. It is erasing their identity. True Tech Equity requires systems that act as Cultural Decoders, learning the unique language of the user's life. The slang. The code words. The family references. The things that only make sense if you know the person's story.

This is why I do what I do. This is why Vista Supports exists. This is why the WATI Institute trains people not just to install technology, but to understand the humans who will be living with it.

Equity requires context. And context requires relationship.

Now let's talk about the frameworks that make sure we're building this right.

The Three Frameworks: Guiding Principles for Building the Ecosystem

So the Enabling Technology Ecosystem is the HOW. It's the structure. It's the approach that gets you to remote supports.

But how do you know if you're building it right? How do you make sure the ecosystem actually serves the person? How do you ensure it's equitable, dignified, and freedom-focused?

That's where my three frameworks come in.

Using my 38 years of experience in the field and what I've learned about transformational systems, I've developed three proprietary frameworks that guide how I build enabling technology ecosystems. They're the principles that ensure we're not just building systems, but building systems that honor humanity.

The Enabled Life Model™ answers the question: What kind of life are we building toward? It defines what a good life looks like across three pillars: Safety, Freedom, and Connection. Before I build an ecosystem for someone, I have to know what we're trying to achieve. This model gives us the vision.

The Tech Equity Triangle™ answers the question: What conditions must exist for technology to be equitable? It defines three requirements that must all be present: Access, Safety, and Liberation. If any one of these is missing, the technology becomes harmful instead of helpful. This framework gives us the ethical foundation.

The Seven Freedoms of ET™ answers the question: What human truths must technology honor? It defines the emotional, cultural, and spiritual dimensions of what technology should restore. These are the freedoms that outdated systems have historically taken from people. This framework gives us the human measure.

Together, these three frameworks create a complete philosophy for human-centered enabling technology. They guide every decision I make when building an ecosystem. They're how I teach others to think about this work. And they're what I'll introduce in the rest of this chapter, then break down fully in Chapter 5.

The Ecosystem is the structure.

The frameworks are the soul.

Let's start with the first one.

SECTION II: The Enabled Life Model™

Reframing Life Through Support, Not Surveillance

For the complete, detailed breakdown of The Enabled Life Model™, see Chapter 5.

Before I can build an enabling technology ecosystem for someone, I have to know what we're building toward. What does a good life look like for this person? What are we actually trying to achieve?

Most conversations about technology in this field start with devices. What sensors should we use? What cameras should we install? What software do we need? But devices are not the point. The point is the LIFE the person gets to live.

The Enabled Life Model™ flips the script. Instead of starting with technology and trying to fit a person into it, this model starts with the human experience and works backward to identify how technology can support that experience.

And it's built on a simple truth:

A good life is a SAFE life, a FREE life, and a CONNECTED life.

Those are the three pillars. Safety. Freedom. Connection. Technology is only as meaningful as the life it protects, expands, and honors. So when I'm building an ecosystem, when I'm thinking about what technology someone needs, I'm always asking: Does this support their safety? Does this expand their freedom? Does this strengthen their connection?

Let me give you a sense of what each pillar means.

Safety: Protection Without Violation

Safety is not about watching people. Safety is about protecting people without violating who they are.

Under this pillar, I'm thinking about predictive support, the kind of technology that sees what the human eye might miss. Technology that can detect changes, alert early, anticipate risk, and prevent crisis before it happens. I'm thinking about crisis reduction, moving from reactive care to proactive care. Fewer ER visits. Fewer "I wish we had known sooner" moments. More stability. More peace. And I'm thinking about health insight, giving people real information about what's happening with their bodies so they have agency over their own lives.

Safety in this model is not surveillance. It's liberating safety. It's protection that preserves dignity.

Freedom: The Purpose of Technology

Freedom is not the opposite of support. Freedom IS support.

Under this pillar, I'm thinking about autonomy, the ability to decide, to choose, to plan, to direct your own life. I'm thinking about privacy, which we treat like a privilege in care systems when it's actually a basic human right. Privacy is adulthood. Privacy is dignity. And I'm thinking about personal control, people being able to control their own environment. Their lights. Their doors. Their temperature. Their space. Simple, everyday control that most of us take for granted.

Technology should make life bigger, not smaller. That's the measure. If a piece of technology restricts someone's freedom, shrinks their world, takes away their choices, then it doesn't belong in this model. The purpose of enabling technology is to expand what's possible for a person, not to limit it.

My grandmother's influence is all over this pillar. Her voice is in every dimension of freedom I teach. "You can do bad all by yourself," she used to say. She meant that independence matters. Dignity matters. Being able to stand on your own two feet, even when you need support, matters.

Connection: The Heart of a Full Life

A person can be safe and free, but without connection, they will not thrive.

Under this pillar, I'm thinking about social belonging, using technology to reduce isolation and support real relationships. I'm thinking about cultural alignment, because technology is not neutral. Technology must match the person's culture, their language, their traditions, their values. What safety means in one community might mean something completely different in another. And I'm thinking about emotional dignity, which is really the soul of this entire model. People want to feel respected, seen, honored, valued, dignified, empowered. If technology reduces dignity, it is not enabling technology. Period.

When I created the Enabled Life Model™, I made culture a required dimension, not an afterthought. That distinction matters more than I can tell you. Because when we ignore culture, we ignore the person. And when we ignore the person, we've already failed.

The Complete Picture

When you put all three pillars together, Safety, Freedom, and Connection, you get a complete picture of what an enabled life looks like. Each pillar has three dimensions within it, nine dimensions total, which I'll break down fully in Chapter 5. But for now, understand this:

An enabled life is not a life filled with devices. It is a life filled with dignity, choice, safety, culture, and connection, supported quietly and respectfully by technology that understands the person, not the system.

This is the vision we're building toward. This is what guides every decision in the ecosystem. This is the Enabled Life Model™, and it is the foundation of everything else in this book.

SECTION III: The Tech Equity Triangle™

The Framework for Systems, States, and Funders

For the complete, detailed breakdown of The Tech Equity Triangle™, see

Chapter 5.

The Enabled Life Model™ tells us what kind of life we're building toward for the person. The Enabling Technology Ecosystem tells us how to build the supports around that person. But here's the question nobody was asking: What has to be in place at the SYSTEMS level for any of this to even be possible?

That's why I created the Tech Equity Triangle™.

This framework is not about the individual. It's about the system. It's about states, funders, policymakers, technology vendors, provider associations, and anyone else who has the power to either open doors or keep them closed. It's the framework that holds systems accountable for creating the conditions where enabling technology can actually work.

Because here's the truth: a person's Enabling Technology Ecosystem is dependent on the system doing its part first. If the system hasn't addressed access, if it hasn't redefined safety, if it hasn't committed to liberation, then the person is stuck. They can want remote supports all day long. Their team can build the most beautiful ecosystem plan you've ever seen. But if the infrastructure isn't there, if the policies don't allow it, if the funding doesn't support it, none of it matters.

The Tech Equity Triangle™ is the pusher. It's what keeps the movement moving.

Access: Has the System Made This Possible?

Access is the foundation of equity. And access is not the person's responsibility. It's the system's responsibility.

Think about a state that wants to become a Tech First State. That sounds great on paper. They put enabling technology in the waiver. They talk about innovation. They encourage providers to explore remote supports. But here's the problem: if that state is largely rural, and most of its members live in areas with no reliable internet, no cell service, dead zones everywhere, then what exactly have they accomplished? They've allowed something that their people can't actually use.

The Tech Equity Triangle™ says that's not good enough. Access means the system has to keep pushing. Work with cell phone service providers. Explore satellite options. Partner with internet companies to expand coverage. Don't just put technology in the waiver and walk away. Make sure your people can actually GET to it.

Access also means affordability. If the technology exists but families can't afford it, that's not access. If the technology exists but it's not available in the languages your members speak, that's not access. If the technology exists but it's not designed for people who are Deaf, blind, or neurodivergent, that's not access.

Technology that only reaches some people is not innovation. It's modern segregation. And the Tech Equity Triangle™ holds systems accountable for closing those gaps.

Safety: Has the System Redefined What Safety Means?

Safety in traditional systems has been about control. Supervision. Monitoring. Compliance. But that definition of safety has caused harm, especially for communities that have historical reasons to distrust systems that claim to be "watching out for them."

The Tech Equity Triangle™ demands that systems redefine safety. Safety is not control. Safety is protection that preserves dignity. And systems have to build that understanding into their policies, their procedures, their training, their oversight.

This means states and funders have to stop confusing surveillance with support. They have to create policies that allow for technology to be used in ways that are trauma-informed, culturally grounded, transparent, and consented to. They have to train their surveyors and auditors to understand the difference between monitoring that protects and monitoring that oppresses.

A camera in one home is support. A camera in another home is harm. Same device. Different meaning. Systems have to be sophisticated enough to understand that difference and create policies that honor it.

Liberation: Is the System Committed to Expanding Freedom?

Liberation is the soul of this framework. And it's the question that separates states that are truly Tech First from states that are just checking a box.

Liberation asks: Is this system actually committed to expanding freedom for the people it serves? Or is technology just being used to make the system more efficient, more comfortable, less liable?

Because technology can go either way. It can expand life or it can shrink it. It can give people more choices or it can give systems more control. The Tech Equity Triangle™ demands that systems commit to the expansion side. Technology should amplify freedom, not replace it.

This means funders have to stop only approving technology that benefits providers. It means states have to measure success not by how many devices are deployed, but by how many lives are expanded. It means policymakers have to ask: Are our people more free because of this technology? Do they have more choices? More dignity? More control over their own lives?

If the answer is no, the system hasn't met the standard of liberation.

Why This Framework Matters for the Movement

The Tech Equity Triangle™ is what gives mission and purpose behind the movement. It's not enough for a state to allow enabling technology in the waiver. That's just the beginning. The Tech Equity Triangle™ keeps pushing. It says: You allowed it, now make it accessible. You made it accessible, now make it safe. You made it safe, now make it liberating.

Access, Safety, and Liberation. All three have to be present at the systems level. If even one is missing, the people who depend on that system will be left behind.

When systems get this right, when they truly commit to all three pillars, they create the conditions where enabling technology ecosystems can thrive. They remove the barriers that have kept people stuck in outdated models. They open doors that have been closed for generations.

And that's when real transformation happens. Not device by device. But system by system. State by state. Policy by policy.

The Tech Equity Triangle™ is how we hold systems accountable for building a future where enabling technology is not a privilege for some, but a possibility for all.

SECTION IV: The Seven Freedoms of ET™

The Human, Emotional, and Cultural Truth Behind Enabling Technology

For the complete, detailed breakdown of The Seven Freedoms of ET™, see Chapter 5.

The Enabled Life Model™ shows us what kind of life we're building toward. The Tech Equity Triangle™ holds systems accountable for making it possible. But why does any of this matter? What are we actually fighting for?

That's what the Seven Freedoms of ET™ answers.

Beneath every conversation about technology, beneath the dashboards, the alerts, the devices, the policies, the strategies, is a human truth that transcends disability, aging, culture, or background: people want to live free. Not free in a symbolic way. Not free in a checkbox way. Free in a way that is felt, lived, embodied, and honored.

The Seven Freedoms of ET™ express the emotional, cultural, and spiritual dimensions of what technology should restore. These are the freedoms that outdated systems have historically taken from people. And these freedoms are the evidence that what we're building is actually working. When you see someone experience these freedoms, you know the ecosystem is functioning. You know the system is changing. You know the vision is becoming real.

This is what should inspire us to continue. This is the heart of the work.

Because enabling technology is not a "tech initiative." It is a human rights movement disguised as a service model.

Freedom 1: Safety Without Surveillance

People want safety, but they do not want to be watched.

This is especially true for Black and Brown communities, for people with trauma histories, for elders who fear institutionalization, for adults with disabilities who have fought their whole lives to be seen as adults, for immigrants with mistrust of government systems, for anyone who has been overcorrected, over-supervised, over-disciplined by systems that claimed to be helping.

Safety without surveillance means being protected without being policed. Being supported without being smothered. Being monitored ethically, respectfully, and consensually. Safety should feel like dignity, not discipline. When technology protects without intruding, when support is present but not oppressive, that is where freedom begins.

Freedom 2: Choice Without Constraint

Every person, whether they have a disability, whether they're aging, or otherwise, deserves the right to choose. Where they live. How they live. What they do. When they sleep. Who they allow in their space. What their day looks like.

Technology should expand choices, not reduce them. In outdated systems, choice is often treated as a privilege. Something you earn. Something that can be taken away. But in an enabled life, choice is treated as a birthright. Choice is the currency of independence.

Freedom 3: Privacy Without Punishment

Privacy is one of the most basic freedoms of adulthood, yet it is often denied to people receiving support.

"I want to be alone" becomes a risk. "I closed my door" becomes an incident. "I need space" becomes a staff meeting. "I want privacy" becomes a debate. But privacy is not a "behavior" to be managed. Privacy is humanity.

Technology can support privacy safely. Non-invasive sensors. Door and environmental alerts. Smart home tools. Supportive remote check-ins. Privacy should never be punished. It should be protected.

Freedom 4: Independence Without Isolation

People want independence, but they do not want to be alone.

This freedom addresses the tension that so many people feel. They want autonomy, but they also want safety. They want space, but they also want connection. They want to be independent, but they also want reassurance that someone is there if they need help.

Technology bridges this tension. Remote supports, communication tools, accessible technology for people who are Deaf or have sensory needs, smart home integration. Independence becomes possible without the fear of isolation. This freedom is essential for aging adults, for adults with disabilities, for people living alone, for families who live far away, for communities facing staffing shortages. Independence must come with connection, not loneliness.

Freedom 5: Identity Without Judgment

Identity is sacred.

Technology must honor race, culture, language, disability identity, gender, neurodivergence, faith, community values, and generational norms. People deserve to be Black without assumptions. Deaf without exclusion. Autistic without being pathologized. Aging without dismissal. Multilingual without barriers. Culturally themselves without being misunderstood. Living with a disability without being treated like a child.

Identity is not a barrier. Identity is dignity. Enabling technology must respect identity, not erase it.

Freedom 6: Control Without Complexity

People want to control their own environment, but they do not want to battle complicated systems to do it.

Technology must be intuitive, accessible, culturally aligned, easy to use, empowering, and responsive. Control looks like setting your own lights. Locking your own doors. Adjusting your own temperature. Communicating your own needs. Managing your own space.

Control is adulthood. Control is safety. Control is self-definition. Technology should make control easier, not harder.

Freedom 7: Joy Without Limitations

Joy is often ignored in care systems, as if the goal is simply to remain alive, not to feel alive.

But joy is culture. Joy is music. Joy is food. Joy is community. Joy is identity and tradition. Joy is laughter and creativity. Joy is dancing. Joy is belonging. And technology, when used correctly, opens doors to joy that systems have historically closed.

Let me tell you a story.

I once supported a young woman who had autism and was adopted from Guatemala. Her life path took her through adoption, foster care, and then independent living with drop-in supports. She was capable. She was intelligent. She had her own apartment and her own life. But she always felt a missing piece. A longing for her Guatemalan identity.

She wanted to learn the dialect of Spanish from her region. She wanted to cook Guatemalan dishes. She wanted to hear the music of her culture, understand the cultural sayings, decorate her home in a way that felt like hers. She wanted to claim a heritage she had lost through no fault of her own.

But no one on her team was Guatemalan. No one spoke her dialect. No one knew her cultural nuances. No one understood the ache she carried.

So we used enabling technology to do something bold and beautiful. I found someone in Guatemala, a person who could connect with her through two-way audio and video, to teach her her own culture. He taught her regional cooking, language, music, traditions, current events, community humor, cultural pride.

And something powerful happened.

She reconnected to a home she had never returned to. And he learned what independence for a woman with a disability looks like in the United States. It was mutual. It was beautiful. It was human.

She regained her joy. Her identity. Her belonging. Her confidence. Her connection to a homeland she thought she had lost forever.

This is what technology can do when it is used with intention, dignity, and imagination. This is joy without limitations.

The Evidence of What We're Building

These seven freedoms are not theoretical. They are emotional truth. Cultural truth. Human truth.

They are the freedoms every person deserves, and the freedoms enabling technology can restore when done with equity and humanity. When you see someone living in safety without surveillance, that's evidence. When you see someone making real choices without constraint, that's evidence. When you see someone experiencing joy without limitations, that's evidence.

This is how we know we're building what we say we're building. This is what should inspire us to continue. This is the heart of everything we do.

Freedom is the outcome. Technology is the tool. Humanity is the center.

This is why we innovate. This is why we lead. This is why this book exists.

SECTION V: What Technology Looks Like When Humanity Leads

If there is one lesson I hope the field never forgets, it is this: Technology cannot lead us. Humanity must lead us. Technology simply follows.

When we lead with fear, technology becomes a barrier. When we lead with humanity, technology becomes a bridge. That distinction matters more than any device, any platform, any innovation we could ever deploy.

COVID Taught Us the Truth

If there was ever a moment that exposed the cracks in our care system, it was COVID. And it didn't expose them gently. It ripped them wide open for everyone to see.

COVID showed us who had access and who didn't. Who had internet and who didn't. Who had options and who was stuck. Who could pivot and who couldn't move. Who had support and who was abandoned. Who had tools and who had nothing. Who the system protected and who the system forgot.

COVID wasn't just a virus. It was the ultimate stress test. And our systems failed. Not because people didn't care, but because the infrastructure was never prepared to evolve. We had built systems that could only work one way, and when that one way became impossible, everything fell apart.

As a society, we were not ready. Families were not ready. Schools were not ready. Providers were not ready. Leadership was not ready. Communities were not ready. Technology platforms were not ready.

And because we were unprepared, children lost years of education. Parents became special education teachers overnight with no training and no support. Adults with disabilities lost services instantly, sometimes with a single phone call saying "we can't come anymore." Elders were isolated and frightened, cut off from the people and routines that gave their lives meaning. Caregivers burned out. Staff refused to leave their homes, and honestly, who could blame them? Communities were cut off from each other. And the most vulnerable people suffered the most. They always do.

Lack of innovation isn't an inconvenience. It's a risk. A real, measurable, life-altering risk.

And While the World Scrambled, We Were Ready

I had been pushing for innovation long before the crisis hit. I had been preparing teams for a shift they didn't yet see coming. I had been advocating for remote supports, smart tools, creative solutions for years. And for years, I heard the same responses: "Not needed." "Not necessary." "We'll cross that bridge when we get there."

Then COVID arrived.

And suddenly, all those "unnecessary" tools became essential. All those conversations people didn't want to have became urgent. All those innovations people said were "nice to have" became the only thing standing between continuity and collapse.

The teams I worked with flipped a switch. Literally. We deployed technology overnight because we had done the work before the emergency. We had the infrastructure. We had the training. We had the relationships. We had the mindset. Not because we were psychic. Not because we knew a pandemic was coming. But because we believed in being ready, not reactive.

Meanwhile, hundreds of providers across the country struggled. They were scrambling to build virtual support systems with no infrastructure, no plans, no training, no tools, no strategy. They were starting from zero in the middle of a crisis.

The difference wasn't luck. It was preparation.

The Most Dangerous Thing We Could Do Now Is Go Back

Some leaders want to return to the way things were. Pre-COVID complacency. Pre-COVID denial. Pre-COVID resistance to technology. They want to pretend we didn't learn what we learned. They want to go back to "normal."

But that's not nostalgia. That's negligence.

We learned the lesson. We survived the test. We saw the consequences with our own eyes. Going back now would be irresponsible. It would be inequitable. It would be dangerous.

Because COVID proved that when crisis hits, systems without technology crumble. And the people who suffer most are always the same people: adults with disabilities, aging adults, families with limited resources, Black and Brown and immigrant communities, foster youth, low-income neighborhoods, people with complex medical needs. The people who were already on the margins get pushed even further out.

We owe them better. We owe them systems that are ready. We owe them innovation that doesn't wait for a crisis to become a priority.

Stay Ready So You Don't Have to Get Ready

I come from the school of "stay ready so you don't have to get ready."

That's not just a saying. That's a philosophy. That's how I've built my entire career. You prepare before the storm, not during it. You build the infrastructure when things are calm so you can deploy it when things get chaotic. You have the hard conversations now so you're not scrambling for answers later.

COVID showed us who was ready and who wasn't. The organizations that had invested in enabling technology, that had built ecosystems, that had trained their teams, that had embraced innovation before they were forced to, those organizations survived. Some of them thrived. They kept people connected. They kept services running. They kept their staff employed and their people supported.

The organizations that had resisted, that had said "we'll deal with that later," that had treated technology as optional, they suffered. Their people suffered. And some of them never recovered.

Tech equity ensures we never face that unprepared again. That's not a nice idea. That's a moral responsibility.

When Humanity Leads the Way Forward

When we lead with humanity, technology becomes the bridge. When we lead with fear, technology becomes the barrier. We get to decide which future we're building.

This chapter is more than theory. It's more than frameworks and definitions. It's a call to action. It's a commitment to build a future where equity, dignity, culture, and freedom lead every decision. Where we prepare before we're forced to. Where we innovate because it's right, not because it's required. Where we put people at the center of everything we build.

Now that we've laid the foundation, now that you understand the Enabling Technology Ecosystem, the Enabled Life Model™, the Tech Equity Triangle™, and the Seven Freedoms of ET™, we step into the rest of this book with clarity, courage, and purpose.

Because the future is here. And we are not going back.

We are building forward.

CHAPTER 3: THE MORAL COMMITMENT

What Tech Equity Demands of Us

Chapter 2 gave you the frameworks. The Enabling Technology Ecosystem. The Enabled Life Model™. The Tech Equity Triangle™. The Seven Freedoms of ET™. Those are the tools. But tools without commitment are just objects sitting on a shelf. They don't change anything by themselves.

This chapter is about what those frameworks demand of you. Not as a professional. Not as someone following regulations. But as a human being.

Because tech equity is not a checklist. It's not a trend. It's not the cool thing to do right now. It's not something you implement because the regulations say you have to or because your state is pushing for innovation. Tech equity is a moral commitment. And if you don't understand that, if you don't feel that in your bones, then nothing I've taught you in this book will matter.

So let me tell you what I mean by moral commitment, and I can only speak for myself in this.

What Moral Commitment Means to Me

I am an advocate. I am someone who truly believes in helping people live their best life. I believe in helping people have opportunities that you and I might take for granted every single day. Opportunities to participate. To give. To take. To share. To love. To learn. To grow. To live.

I'm also a woman of color. So I understand what it means to not always get easy access to opportunity. I understand what it means to work hard, and sometimes harder than the person standing beside me who doesn't look like me, just so my divine gifts can be utilized. I understand what it feels like to have to prove yourself in rooms where your presence is questioned before you even open your mouth.

And because I understand that, I understand something else too: a disability doesn't make you unequal. But the opportunities are unequal. The access is unequal. The seats at the table are unequal. The voices that get heard are unequal.

So when I talk about making a moral commitment, I'm talking about committing to change that. I'm committing to make sure that people are not X'd out. Not overlooked. Not made invisible. Not seen as less than. I'm committing to inclusion. To community inclusion. To listening. To making sure that people with disabilities, aging adults, families, caregivers, and communities that have been left out for too long are finally seen as equals. Because they always were equals. The system just didn't treat them that way.

The Responsibility of Having a Seat

Here's what I believe, and maybe it doesn't resonate with everyone, but it resonates with me:

Anyone who has the ability to speak, anyone who has the opportunity to be in a room with listeners, anyone who has a seat at any table, has a moral obligation to bring along those who aren't in that room.

Whether or not you agree with that, I need you to at least think about it. Think about where you are right now. Think about the opportunities you've been given. And I'm not just talking about people in positions of obvious privilege. Wherever you are could be a place of advantage or a place of disadvantage. But wherever you are, you have an opportunity. And the question is: what are you doing with it?

Are you using your voice to speak for those who don't have the same voice? Are you using your platform, however big or small, to bring others along? Are you representing the people you serve, or are you just representing yourself?

Some people might think this sounds lofty. Maybe it doesn't make sense to everybody. But it makes sense to me. And from where I come from, it makes a heck of a lot of sense.

I love seeing people who came from where I came from, or who look similar to the way I look, in places of influence. I love hearing someone speak on my behalf, even if they don't know me personally, because it makes me feel seen. And being seen matters. It matters more than most people realize. Because there are so many people who are made invisible by systems, by assumptions, by neglect, by indifference. And when someone finally sees them, when someone finally speaks for them, when someone finally says "you matter and I'm going to make sure this room knows it," that changes something. It changes everything.

Who I'm Talking To

So let me be specific about who I'm talking to, because this moral commitment applies to everyone who touches this work.

If you're a funder, you're in a position to make sure these voices get heard. Equally heard. You're in a position to represent the people who depend on the decisions you make. Now, whether or not the people above you see it that way, whether or not the people who vote on funding share your values, I still believe your job is to present those you're representing. You have a seat. Use it.

If you're a parent, and you have the ability to speak up, to advocate, to be in rooms where decisions are made, then you're speaking on behalf of all parents. Including the ones who don't have the same opportunities you have. The ones who can't take off work to attend the meeting. The ones who don't speak English fluently. The ones who don't know the system well enough to navigate it. You're their voice too.

If you're an advocate, or a person working in disability services, or a caregiver for a senior or an elderly person, you have a seat. You see things that others don't see. You know things that others don't know. You have the opportunity to speak up for the people you serve. That's not optional. That's the responsibility that comes with the work.

If you're a nurse working in a hospital, if you're a doctor, if you're a clinician of any kind, you have influence. You have credibility. You have the ability to say "this matters" and have people listen. What are you doing with that?

If you're a leader in this field, if you're making decisions about technology, about policy, about funding, about implementation, then the moral commitment is even heavier. Because the decisions you make don't just affect you. They affect people who will never be in the room with you. People who will never know your name. People whose lives will be shaped by choices they had no say in.

That's the weight of leadership. And if you're not willing to carry it with integrity, with humanity, with a commitment to the people you serve, then you shouldn't be in the seat.

What This Looks Like in Practice

I know this might sound like a dream. But I am the Chief Innovation and Dream Officer. Dreams are what I do.

And here's what I dream about: What would it look like if we all took our individualized privilege, meaning our opportunities, no matter how high or low that opportunity is, and used it to speak on behalf of those who don't have the same opportunity? What would it look like if everyone who had a voice used that voice for someone else? What would it look like if every room, every meeting, every decision included the perspective of the people most affected, even when they couldn't be there themselves?

I don't know. Maybe I'm crazy. But to me, it sounds like the right thing to do. It sounds like what care should actually look like. It sounds like what community should be. It sounds like what we're supposed to be building.

The Connection to Tech Equity

This is why tech equity matters. Not because it's innovative. Not because it's efficient. Not because the regulations are moving in this direction. Tech equity matters because it's about dignity. It's about liberation. It's about justice. It's about making sure that people who have been overlooked, underserved, and made invisible finally have access to the tools, the supports, and the opportunities that can change their lives.

The frameworks I gave you in Chapter 2 are powerful. But they're only powerful if you use them with this commitment in your heart. If you implement technology without caring about the people it's supposed to serve, you're just digitizing the same old harm. If you build ecosystems without asking who's being left out, you're building systems of exclusion with better equipment. If you talk about innovation without talking about justice, you're missing the point entirely.

Tech equity is not the future. Tech equity is the foundation. And without this moral commitment underneath it, nothing we build will last. Nothing we build will matter. Nothing we build will deserve to be called "care."

So I'm asking you, whoever you are, wherever you sit, whatever seat you have: What are you going to do with your opportunity?

Are you going to use it for yourself? Or are you going to use it to bring others along?

The frameworks are ready. The tools are ready. The question is: Are you ready to make the commitment?

Because this work requires more than knowledge. It requires more than skills. It requires heart. It requires conscience. It requires a willingness to see people who have been made invisible and say, "I see you. And I'm going to make sure others see you too."

That's the moral commitment. That's what tech equity demands. And that's what this book is really about.

CHAPTER 4: CULTURE, COMMUNITY & TECHNOLOGY: WHY REPRESENTATION MATTERS

The System Was Never Built With Us in Mind

Let's begin with a truth many feel but few will say out loud: most care systems were not built with culture in mind. Not Black culture. Not Brown culture. Not Deaf culture. Not immigrant culture. Not neurodivergent culture. Not LGBTQ+ culture. Not disability culture. Not aging culture.

These systems were created from Western norms, white middle-class values, clinical frameworks, institutional models, paternalistic assumptions, rigid hierarchy, and risk-averse thinking. And because culture was never part of the foundation, technology built within these systems carries the same blind spots.

Technology inherits the worldview of whoever designed it.

So when people say, "I don't trust the technology," what they often mean is, "I don't trust the system that created it." Because if the system has historically surveilled you, misunderstood you, erased you, punished you, ignored your boundaries, denied your autonomy, pathologized your identity, and misread your communication, why would you trust its devices?

Technology is not neutral. Technology reflects culture. And culture shapes trust.

When Protection Becomes Disconnection: The Oxtail Story

Let me tell you a story about how the system's best intentions can disconnect people from the very things that make life worth living.

I used to work at an ICF in upstate New York. In this particular setting, there were three siblings from Colombia. They had come to the States looking for a better life. Two of the young ladies didn't communicate with verbal words. They used paper keyboards on their lap trays and physical cues. And let me tell you, you could have a full conversation with them.

Now, I understand why regulations exist around food and nutrition. I get it. My husband and I live together, and his idea of a nutritious meal is way different than my definition of a nutritious meal. So I understand the need for universal practices and approaches to nutritional value. We want to make sure people are getting their nutrients. Got it.

However, at times, the system doing the very right thing could very well be limiting a person from experiencing their best life. Their best cultural life.

The house had a chef. He was Korean, trained on cooking nutritious meals. And the menu was the menu. I knew every month, for that season, what we were eating. It's Tuesday, we're eating pasta with oyster sauce or whatever. We knew the whole menu.

But one day, we were all just sitting at the kitchen table, chatting like a family. And I started talking about how over the weekend I was going to make some oxtails. Cola de vaca. I'm describing how I'm going to make them, and all of a sudden, one of the young ladies starts responding. Stretching. Looking at me. Moving her arm in a way that said, "I got something to say."

I said, "What? What do you have to say?"

So she starts spelling on her paper lap keyboard. She wanted some.

Now, this young lady was on a G-tube feeding. Pureed foods. Some foods by mouth. Her sister too. Their brother couldn't have anything by mouth at all. But they were all getting excited.

I said, "What do you know about oxtail? What do you know about cola de vaca?"

And she just got so excited. Her face lit up. And I need you to understand something. This was not a person who normally had a lot of smiles on her face. But on that particular day, they were all smiling. So happy.

I said, "You want me to bring the oxtails in?"

Now I'm trying to figure out how I'm going to get those oxtails to be in the consistency she can eat. Normally, you're not allowed to bring any food from outside to feed anybody. Just another restriction that the regulations, in their attempt to protect, were actually preventing. But we worked it out. Between me, the chef, the house manager, the nutritionist, we figured it out.

I made the oxtails. And I remembered to pack all of the sauce and the juices because I knew we had to get this thing pureed down. Nurse Jane was there. We got that oxtail pureed down to the smoothest consistency. And then she typed on her lapboard: "Put some juice in the Ensure."

She wanted it mixed. The oxtail juice mixed with her Ensure, the liquid nutritional supplement she got three times a day.

We looked at each other. Are we sure we can mix that? Nurse Jane said it's a liquid, it's a liquid, it should be fine, same consistency. Let's blend it up. Let's see what it looks like. Because according to the GI doctor and the nutritionist, even though it's going in the G-tube, most people can still taste. Even hours afterwards.

So we did it. We pureed it down. We mixed it. And we gave it to her.

When I tell you. The way she closed her eyes. The way she marinated on that taste. At that moment, food wasn't just about human survival. It wasn't just eating to stay alive, which she did every day, no problem. But the way she closed her eyes and held it in her mouth. You could see her experiencing the food.

Because for a lot of cultures, especially in Black, Brown, and Latino communities, food is life. Food is memory. Food has so many cultural connections and people connections. Even just me talking about oxtails right now, Francena Brown is coming into my head because it's connected. When I say oxtails, lots of memories come up. I think about my bonus family in Colombia. I think about when my God-sister, who I call Mamita, makes me oxtails when I'm in my second home in Colombia. That's how food is experienced. It's love. It's joy. It's culture.

It's connection.

And in that moment, what I saw and witnessed was this: part of our responsibility is making sure culture is represented in service delivery models. While we are doing our best to provide protection and make sure people get healthy, nutritious meals, we could actually be disconnecting people from experiences of life that they would enjoy, that they want to carry with them. We disconnect them when we don't consider meals that are connected to their life, their family, their culture.

Because those things matter. Having them represented in your today matters.

When Community Inclusion Destroys Community: Susie's Story

Here's another story about how systems set up to do the right thing can cause harm when we don't consider what people lose along the way.

I used to work at a place that had a sheltered workshop. People would do employment there. They had government contracts, corporate contracts. I remember one contract where they were putting together pieces for a very high luxury brand. Another contract where they were putting together letters that would go on a luxury car. But they didn't get paid the same way they would if they worked in a different kind of establishment.

At some point, the system said we need to close sheltered workshops and make sure people are gainfully employed in competitive employment. Great. I fully agree with that. I'm not defending sheltered workshops.

But I want to talk about what happened to Susie.

Susie worked in the sheltered workshop, and she lived in a very large group home. We're talking 15, 16 people at the time. And she's working in this workshop where she's got all kinds of friends. Regardless of the situation with the pay, she had a community. She had herself a boyfriend in there too.

Every day she came to work, not only was she making a little something, but she was getting to spend time with her boyfriend. They would have lunch together on the lunch break. Maybe they were shooting each other eyes all day long, I don't know. But they had lunch together every single day. And in her very large group home, she also had friends. People she lived with. People she watched TV with. People she laughed with.

Then the right decision came. Sheltered workshops were closed down. Large group homes were separated.

Susie got a job working at a local department store, in the warehouse. She was given a smaller apartment with just her and one other roommate, in the community.

And from that point forward, everyone started to notice depression.

Because at the end of the day, while she did go out into what we would consider to be "the community," she lost connection to HER community. She no longer saw her boyfriend every day at work. She went from seeing him every day to seeing him whenever she could. She no longer had the same community she lived with because she now lived with just one other person. She missed everybody sitting down, watching the same show, laughing about it, talking about it. She lost that community.

Here's what I'm saying: making sure people have access to the community is a good thing. But we didn't consider how to maintain those connections when we were making these changes.

I hear a lot of people who used to be in Letchworth Village or Forest Haven. A lot of them who have the ability to communicate or articulate what it was like will tell you two things: "It was awful. But I had a lot of friends that I knew."

It was awful. But I had a lot of friends.

There's something to learn from that. When we develop systems, we often exclude the very people those systems are supposed to serve from the conversation. We don't ask them what they'll lose. We don't consider what matters to them. We just decide what's best and move forward.

And then we wonder why there's depression. Why there's resistance. Why people don't seem grateful for the "improvement" we gave them.

Community is not just geography. Community is not just living in a neighborhood instead of an institution. Community is the people you love. The people who know you. The people you see every day. The people you laugh with.

And if our systems destroy that in the name of "community inclusion," we haven't included anyone in anything. We've just moved the isolation to a different address.

When Meaning Is Personal: The Dean Martin Story

One of the most important lessons I've learned in this work is that there is no universal human experience. And technology must honor the meaning each person assigns to the world.

I was recently talking with some peers within a technology collaborative. We were discussing AI and its ability to flex for people with cognitive disabilities. The question came up: Can AI pick up on words? If somebody says "I'm depressed," could that trigger the system to call someone who could call back, talk to them, maybe run through their behavior support plan?

And they said, yes, of course. We were able to work through that scenario. Made sense.

But then I said, well, what if the person said something like "Dean Martin"?

They looked at me confused.

Let me explain. I worked with a woman, a friend, who has a cognitive disability. And at the trigger of one word, one specific phrase, a situation could turn into a situation I don't even want to get into. For those in the field, we might call it maladaptive behaviors. I say that just to cover it because I don't want to tell all her business.

But her trigger word was Dean Martin.

Now, to AI, to most technology, "Dean Martin" is a singer. A Hollywood icon. Classic entertainment. A light conversation topic. If you said "Dean Martin" to AI, it would probably start thinking that was a trigger to have a conversation about the actor, about movies, about the Rat Pack, about all this other stuff.

But to her? Dean Martin was loaded with emotion, history, and personal meaning that had nothing to do with any of that. One phrase, two entirely different worlds.

And when I explained this, it brought some light to them. Because when working with people with intellectual and developmental disabilities, you have to understand that they have their own unique interpretation of the same world that we all live in.

Whereas I might say "I'm depressed" and the technology would be supportive of me because I said a universal word, just like there's a universal sign for choking, just like we have in the non-disability world, different cultures interpret different things differently. In her case, that technology would miss her trigger word completely because it was not created to accept alternatives to the universal language.

Now here's what I need you to understand. This is not just a lesson about people with IDD. This is not just a cultural lesson. This is a lesson on humanity.

We all create and learn from our lifespan different ways we interpret the same land that we are standing on. What makes us so beautiful is our ability to share and understand those differences so that we, uniquely as a whole, can create this beautiful thing we call human beings.

Meaning is personal. Meaning is identity. Meaning is culture. And if technology cannot interpret personal meaning, it cannot claim to be equitable.

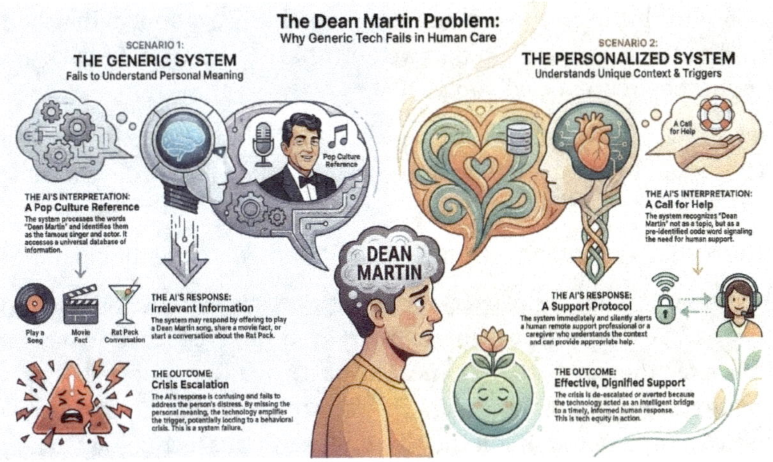

The Dean Martin Problem: Why Generic Tech Fails in Human Care — Scenario 1 (Generic System) vs. Scenario 2 (Personalized System)

Why We Keep Having to Go Back and Get People

I need to say something that might be uncomfortable, but it's the truth.

Right now, I am promoting digital inclusion. I'm talking about tech equity. I'm writing this book. But I'm talking about it after the fact. After all of us have already arrived. After we've already decided whether or not we want to be involved with technology. After we've had access to whatever cell phone we want. You got people walking around with iPhone 17 Pro Max. You got people still holding onto their Blackberries by a thin, thin thread.

But the point is, we already had access.

So when I'm writing this book to encourage tech equity, to encourage inclusion in the digital community, to encourage the use of technology in everyday life like the rest of us, I'm going backwards to bring people up on something that's already happening.

And what I dream, and here I go with these dreams again, but I'm going to keep having these dreams as a Dream Officer, what I dream is that we stop excluding people along the way. That we stop leaving them out from the beginning. So that we don't have to keep going back and bringing them up to catch up.

They should always be considered when everything else is happening. They should be right along with us from the start. Why is it always an afterthought?

And see, that afterthought brings harm. Whether it's intentional or not.

Right now, I'm having conversations with people who use technology every day. People who probably couldn't even survive life without some piece of technology in their home. Maybe it's that Ring doorbell they're using to monitor their teenager. They're not even using it for what it's supposed to be used for. But they have access to this technology to help them do something they wouldn't be able to do otherwise.

And that same person is debating with me about whether or not technology would be valuable for people with disabilities.

You see, when we don't consider them first, we use too much of our energy, time, and vocabulary to keep them excluded. Whether it's intentional or not.

This is why I've elevated my level of advocacy. This is why I'm writing this book. When I'm at tech events, I make it a point to go to mainstream technology summits, not just the disability-specific conferences. Yes, CES has sections about assistive technology and age tech. But CES is not a disability-only event. It's one of the biggest consumer electronics shows in the world. And that's exactly why I go.

I go to places where the disability community is not the majority. I go to represent. To advocate. To have dialogue about the needs of people with cognitive disabilities with vendors and innovators who might not be thinking about them at all.

I'm asking the question: When you made this device, did you remember them? Can you remember them when you modify it? How can we utilize it for somebody who has this need?

Because here's what bothers me. I don't remember the last time I physically went to the grocery store. Now, I don't have a disability that prevents me from going. I have a thing called I don't like the grocery store and I'm lazy. Technology is what gets my groceries in the house.

If I can do that, and I don't have any disability that prevents me from going to the grocery store, think about the person who does have a disability and really can't make it to the store. And yet we haven't given them access to order their groceries on their own using that same technology. Because we believe that we should be the ones in between them and their groceries.

That's stupid to me.

But we need to start thinking about these things. Even the military says no airman, no soldier, nobody left behind. But for some reason, when it comes to technology, it's a debate about whether or not it has value for people with disabilities. When we ourselves are using it for the simplest little things in our lives.

Representation Is Not Optional

So let me bring this all together.

Technology without representation is incomplete. Technology without culture is ineffective. Technology without equity is unethical.

Representation is not about diversity optics. Representation is about understanding humanity. Respecting identity. Honoring culture. Designing with people, not for them. Seeing what systems have ignored. Bridging what institutions have broken. Being accountable to the communities served.

This is about human safety. Emotional dignity. Cultural belonging. Liberation.

When I think about that young woman closing her eyes, marinating on the taste of oxtails, I think about what we almost denied her. When I think about Susie losing her boyfriend, her friends, her community, I think about what we took from her in the name of "inclusion." When I think about the woman whose trigger word was Dean Martin, I think about how much we assume we understand when we understand so little.

And when I think about all the people who are still waiting for us to go back and get them, I think about how we could have brought them along from the beginning if we had just remembered they existed.

Representation is innovation. Culture is innovation. Equity is innovation.

And nothing truly "enabling" can exist without all three.

The moral commitment I talked about in Chapter 3, using your seat, using your voice, bringing others along, this is where it shows up. This is where it becomes real. In the food we serve. In the communities we protect or destroy. In the technology we build or withhold. In the questions we ask or don't ask.

Culture is not a barrier to technology. Culture is the key to technology.

And until we understand that, until we feel that, until we build with that truth at the center, we will keep creating systems that harm the people they're supposed to serve.

We can do better. We have to do better.

And it starts with remembering that every person we serve has a culture, a community, a history, and a meaning that belongs to them. Our job is not to erase that. Our job is to honor it.

That's what representation means. That's what culture demands. And that's what this work is really about.

CHAPTER 5: THE FRAMEWORKS: BUILDING BLOCKS FOR HUMAN-CENTERED ENABLING TECHNOLOGY

The Enabled Life Model™, The Tech Equity Triangle™, and The Seven Freedoms of ET™

In Chapter 2, I introduced you to my three frameworks. I gave you the overview, the foundation, the why behind each one. But this chapter is different. This chapter is the deep dive. This is where we go beneath the surface and really understand what these frameworks mean in practice.

Because frameworks on paper don't change anything. Frameworks in action change everything.

So let me take you deeper.

WHY I BUILT THESE FRAMEWORKS

For decades, this field has talked about technology in one of two ways.

The first way is device-first. What gadgets can we buy? What sensors should we install? What's the latest technology? This approach treats technology like a shopping list. It misses the human entirely.

The second way is fear-first. What if it fails? What about privacy? People don't want to be monitored. This approach treats technology like a threat to be managed. It also misses the human entirely.

Neither approach centers the person. Neither approach asks the most important question: What does a full, dignified, empowered life look like, and how can technology support it?

That's the question I've been answering for 38 years. And these frameworks are how I answer it.

The Enabled Life Model™ answers: What does a dignified life look like when technology is supporting, not replacing, human care?

The Tech Equity Triangle™ answers: What conditions must exist at the systems level for technology to be equitable and just?

The Seven Freedoms of ET™ answers: What emotional and human truths must technology honor?

Together, these three frameworks create a complete philosophy for human-centered enabling technology. They are simple enough to remember, deep enough to guide practice, flexible enough to apply in any setting, and powerful enough to transform systems.

And they are mine. Not because I'm claiming territory, but because no one else has articulated them. The field needed language for what we're building. So I created it.

Now let me show you what they really mean.

FRAMEWORK 1: THE ENABLED LIFE MODEL™

A 3×3 Framework for Human-Centered, Tech-Enabled Living

This model answers the most important question in this entire book: What does a full, dignified, empowered life look like when technology is supporting, not replacing, human care?

Most conversations about enabling technology start with devices. What sensors? What cameras? What software? But devices are not the point. The point is the LIFE the person gets to live.

The Enabled Life Model™ flips the script. It starts with the human experience and works backward to identify how technology can support that experience.

The model sits on three foundational pillars that represent the full human experience: Safety, Freedom, and Connection. Each pillar has three dimensions, a total of nine dimensions that define what an enabled life really looks like.

Because I'm not building a model for devices. I'm building a model for dignity, culture, and possibility.

PILLAR 1: SAFETY

Not Surveillance. Not Control. Not Fear. Safety That Empowers.

Let me be clear about what safety means in this model.

Safety is not constant surveillance. It's not cameras in every room. It's not someone watching your every move. It's not control disguised as protection. It's not fear-based restrictions.

Safety is secure independence. It's predictable support. It's early warning without intrusion. It's protection that preserves dignity. It's peace of mind for the person AND their loved ones.

Safety in the Enabled Life Model™ is about empowerment, not control.

Dimension 1: Predictive Support

Technology that anticipates needs and risks without limiting autonomy.

This includes motion sensors that detect unusual patterns, fall detection systems, nighttime monitoring for wandering, medication reminders, environmental alerts when a stove is left on or a door is left open. The goal is to prevent harm while preserving dignity.

Predictive support says: I see a potential problem, and I'm alerting someone who can help before it becomes a crisis.

This is the difference between waiting for someone to fall and break a hip, and noticing they've been unsteady for three days and intervening early. Prediction prevents crisis.

Dimension 2: Crisis Reduction

Proactive, tech-enabled systems that reduce avoidable ER visits, hospitalizations, behavioral escalations, medical emergencies, and dangerous situations. The goal is stabilization over reaction.

Most care systems are reactive. Something happens, then we respond. Crisis reduction flips that model. Technology provides continuous data that allows teams to see patterns early. Sleep is disrupted for five nights, intervene before exhaustion leads to crisis. Vital signs are shifting, consult with the doctor before hospitalization is needed. Activity is declining, check in before depression sets in.

Safety is not about control. It's about stabilization.

Dimension 3: Health Insight

Technology that gives people, families, and providers information early enough to act. This includes vitals monitoring, sleep pattern tracking, activity data, wellness trends, and baseline comparisons. The goal is health literacy and health equity through technology.

For too long, medical decisions for people with disabilities have been based on staff memory, inconsistent documentation, "they seem off today," and guesswork. Health insight changes that. Now we have real data.

When a doctor asks, "How has their sleep been?" we don't have to guess. We have the data. When a nurse asks, "Have their vitals changed?" we can show trends, not approximations. Health insight is equity. It's giving people access to the same quality of health information that everyone deserves.

PILLAR 2: FREEDOM

The Heart of the Enabled Life Model™

Freedom is not optional in this model. Freedom is the PURPOSE of technology.

Too many systems treat freedom as a risk to be managed. What if they fall? What if something happens? What if they make a bad decision? But freedom is not the enemy of safety. Freedom IS safety.

When people have control over their lives, privacy in their homes, autonomy in their decisions, and tools that support independence, they are safer than when we strip those things away. Freedom reduces harm. Control increases it.

Let me tell you a story that shows what freedom really looks like when technology gets it right.

The Meta Glasses Story: When We Get Out of the Way

I was working with a young woman who was pretty independent. She could do a lot of things on her own. She received drop-in support, not 24-hour staffing. But she refused almost every medical appointment. And I mean almost every single one.

Now, for the agency, that's a problem. We're responsible for making sure she's healthy and safe. We have to check our boxes. Regulatory-wise, we could get in trouble if she's not going to her appointments.

But here's what nobody was asking: WHY was she refusing?

So let me give you the backdrop. When she did go to appointments, we sent staff with her. The DSP or the nurse would go into the room with her. And here's what would happen: the doctor, who already sees her diagnosis, who already sees she has a cognitive disability, would automatically start talking to the staff person. Not to her. To the staff.

It's not that doctors do this on purpose. It's just something that naturally happens. You show up with staff, and the doctor thinks, I need to talk to the staff. Otherwise, why are they here?

I think about when I was a teenager, starting to age out of my pediatrician. The doctor was asking questions, but he was asking my mother. And I remember thinking, she doesn't know. At this point I'm leaving the house, going to school by myself, living a whole life she doesn't know about. But the doctor's talking to her like she has all the answers.

And I remember the next time I needed to go to the doctor, I told her I didn't want her to go with me. But of course, this is a Black mama. She got my insurance card, she got all my access, she got everything. So you need to ask her for permission. And that comes with a whole bunch of questions.

Now, I was a quote-unquote normal functioning teenager just trying to express my authentic, independent self. But my mother, who in this case would be my staff, was not trying to hear that.

The point is this: when I'm in an appointment, there may be things I want to talk to my doctor about. But I don't need another person hearing it. That could be my mother, my husband, a friend, my sister. I don't care. I want to talk to my doctor by myself, and I want him to talk to ME. Not talk around me. Not talk at me as if I don't understand.

The same thing happens to people with disabilities who have the capability of communicating with their doctor. But you have this staff person sitting there, so the doctor relays all the information to the staff instead of to the patient. The actual patient, whose appointment it is, gets completely ignored.

That is like torture. And that is whack.

Why would she ever want to go to an appointment and be totally invisible?

So she said, you know what, I'm not going.

Now we had a problem to solve. She was expressing that she wanted autonomy. She wanted independence. She didn't want us in her appointment. But she was also telling me she sometimes didn't understand what the doctor said, or she forgot to get the prescription, or she needed some assistance. She just didn't need us blocking her relationship with her doctor.

So what did we do?

We got her some smart glasses. Meta glasses with clear lenses. We connected them to her iPhone. She's a young woman, so she's already got her phone in her hand all the time. Nobody thinks anything of it. It's not a courtroom, so she can have her phone.

We could escort her from her apartment, help her travel in the community, make sure she got on the right bus to get to her appointment. And while she was in the doctor's office, we could remind her through the glasses to get the script, to get the order for the lab. But we weren't

IN the room.

And here's what happened.

The doctor didn't see a staff person. He only saw her. So now the doctor is talking directly to her. Having a relationship with his patient. Actually SEEING her.

She is seen. That is the most important part.

If we're talking about community inclusion, about building relationships, about being part of the community, then she needs to have the relationship with her doctor. Not me. Even if that doctor was also my doctor, my community and her community do not mix. She needs the connection with him in her space. She needs to feel comfortable to talk to her doctor. She needs to be able to hit the mute button when she doesn't want us to hear what she's saying. That's her right.

You can't hit mute on a person sitting in the room with you.

We had to convince her service coordinator. We had to convince everybody that she was healthy and safe with this approach. The service coordinator was down with it, but they also represent the oversight agency, so there were conversations.

But after everyone saw the data, after they saw that she was no longer "non-compliant" with her medical appointments, that she was now 100% compliant, they understood. Why was she compliant now? Because she was heard. Because she was seen.

This is what freedom looks like. We found a way to get out of the way and still provide the support and the safety without the surveillance.

That's Dimension 4, 5, and 6 all working together.

Dimension 4: Autonomy

Technology that lets individuals make their own decisions, live alone or semi-independently, self-direct their care, move freely in their environment, and manage their own space. The goal is that technology becomes the tool of independence.

Autonomy means I decide when I wake up. I decide what I eat. I decide who enters my home. I decide how I spend my day. Technology supports autonomy by providing tools that extend capability, offering backup without requiring constant presence, giving people control over their environment, and respecting choices even when others disagree.

Autonomy is adulthood. Technology protects it.

Dimension 5: Privacy

This is the dimension the system always misses.

People don't want staff in their space constantly. They don't want supervision masquerading as support. They don't want someone watching them 24/7. Privacy is one of the most basic freedoms of adulthood. And yet, for people receiving support, privacy is often treated as a risk, a privilege, something to be earned, or a "behavior" to be addressed.

"I want to be alone" becomes an incident report. "I closed my door" becomes a safety concern. "I need space" becomes a team meeting.

This is wrong. Privacy is not a behavior. Privacy is humanity.

Technology can support privacy safely through non-invasive sensors, door alerts instead of staff checks, environmental monitoring without visual surveillance, and remote check-ins that are scheduled, not random.

Privacy should never be punished. It should be protected.

Dimension 6: Personal Control

Technology that people can actually operate. Smart lights they can control. Smart locks they can manage. Smart thermostats they can adjust. Voice assistants that respond to them. Communication tools that work for them. Doorbell cameras they can access.

When people can control their environment, they control their lives.

Control looks like setting your own lights, locking your own doors, adjusting your own temperature, communicating your own needs, managing your own space.

Control is adulthood. Control is safety. Control is self-definition. The Enabled Life Model™ recognizes that control belongs to the person. Technology just makes it easier.

PILLAR 3: CONNECTION

Humanity Must Stay at the Center

Technology is not a replacement for human connection. Technology is a bridge TO human connection. The Enabled Life Model™ requires emotional, cultural, and relational connection. Because a life with safety and freedom but no connection is still an empty life.

Let me tell you another story.

The Woman with 100 Questions: When Technology Fills the Gap

There are some things we in the IDD field don't really talk about much, or maybe it sounds awful to actually say out loud. But these are real things, and technology can be an assistance.

Human beings are human beings. We get tired and frustrated. Even the sweetest person can get tired. Even the most helpful doctor can get frustrated. Even the best childcare provider can be sick of kids at one point. Because we're human.

Mothers. My mother loves us. But I can't even count how many times she said, "Y'all are getting on my nerves." And a mother's love is undefeated. A mother's love is almost superhuman when it comes to protecting her child. Even a mother can say, I need a break from these kids.

DSPs are superheroes. But they're also human. And we overwork them. Our field overworks whoever shows up to work. We have a workforce crisis. Truth be told, we always had a workforce crisis. But it's getting worse. You don't have a lot of people signing up voluntarily to do this type of work. So those who show up get overworked. And overworked means their patience grows thin.

They love what they do. I know so many passionate, loving DSPs. People I would call with a drop of the dime if I needed help. But they can grow weary and tired too.

Now imagine you've been working 48-hour shifts. Not saying that's legal. Just imagine. And you now have a person who's excited to see you on shift, and they have a lot of questions.

I think about my nieces and nephews when they were small. The amount of questions a three, four, five-year-old has is incredible. Somebody should write a book about it. They can ask so many questions back to back to back. And I love them. But they can wear you thin. I remember just answering with mm-hmms and uh-huhs, trying to get something to occupy their time so they'd stop asking me questions.

This happens in our field. We have people we support who ask a lot of questions. Repetitive questions. And the staff are tired. The staff are worn out.

I was working at a home where there was a woman who asked maybe 100 questions per hour. And she waited for the response. If you said the same thing you said before, it frustrated her. But you might have been so weary that you didn't have any more answers to give her differently. And she had a great memory. She would tell you, "You said that yesterday." And she expected you to come up with something new.

It's difficult. But here's what she was really saying: I want to have a conversation where we keep progressing. I want to have an intellectual conversation where we don't repeat the same thing from before. I would like to elevate my level of thinking.

Well, maybe in my human mortal body, I was not smart enough or strong enough or wise enough to meet her expectations.

Enter AI.

We set it up so she could get that level of intellect. That level of intelligence. Artificial or not, it was doing better than me. She would ask it questions, and they would have full-fledged, genius-level conversations about all different topics. To the point that she wore herself out.

This is where technology has meaning for both parties. She got the level of genius she wanted. The staff weren't getting frustrated because they couldn't reach that level. Win-win.

It was amazing to watch. I sat there thinking, wow, that's really a deep conversation. I was intrigued by it. But she wasn't limited by my personal limitations.

Sometimes we think we are the end-all be-all to someone's level of growth. To someone's level of independence. That's the furthest thing from the truth. Someone's only limited because maybe the people around them are limited. Maybe the opportunities have been limited. Maybe the skill levels of the people around them are limited. Or the way we think is limited.

Someone else's limited life should not limit someone else's life.

If I don't have any more to give, I should not tell her that her dream is not valid. I should not try to dumb down her expectations. That's what I call being a dream enabler. Thinking outside of my own limitations so that she can experience her full life.

That's what the Connection pillar is about.

Dimension 7: Social Belonging

Technology that prevents isolation and strengthens relationships. Virtual family check-ins, accessible communication tools, social apps and platforms, video calls with loved ones, communication tools accessible for people who are Deaf, sensory-friendly connection tools.

The goal is simple: everyone deserves community. Isolation is deadly. It leads to depression, cognitive decline, health deterioration, loss of will to live. Technology fights isolation by keeping people connected to family, enabling new friendships, providing access to communities of interest, and making communication possible across distances.

Social belonging is a human need. Technology can protect it.

Dimension 8: Cultural Alignment

This is where I stand alone.

Technology must fit culture, language, identity, values, history, personal meaning, community traditions, and generational norms. Technology is not neutral.

A sensor designed for a suburban white family may not work for a Black elder with historical trauma around surveillance. It may not work for a Deaf person who needs visual alerts, not audio. It may not work for a Spanish-speaking immigrant who can't read English interfaces. It may not work for a person with autism who is triggered by certain sounds.

Cultural alignment means technology adapts to the person, not the other way around.

When I created the Enabled Life Model™, I made culture a required dimension, not an afterthought. This is my intellectual innovation. It's what makes this framework different from anything else in the field.

If technology doesn't fit the culture, the culture will reject the technology.

Dimension 9: Emotional Dignity

Technology that protects pride, self-worth, confidence, spiritual comfort, and identity. The goal is that people are not data points. They are humans deserving of dignity.

This dimension is unique to this model. It's emotional. It's rooted in Black experiences, Brown experiences, immigrant experiences, marginalized experiences.

Emotional dignity means technology doesn't make you feel less than. Technology doesn't strip your identity. Technology doesn't reduce you to a problem to be monitored. Technology honors your full humanity.

Emotional dignity is the soul of the Enabled Life Model™.

THE COMPLETE MODEL

The Enabled Life Model™: A 3×3 Framework

Visualize a 3×3 grid, like a tic-tac-toe board. Each column represents one of the three pillars: Safety, Freedom, Connection. Each row contains the three dimensions that define what that pillar means in practice.

The Enabled Life Model™: A Framework for Dignity, Freedom, and Connection

PILLAR 1: SAFETY: Predictive Support, Crisis Reduction, Health Insight

PILLAR 2: FREEDOM: Autonomy, Privacy, Personal Control

PILLAR 3: CONNECTION: Social Belonging, Cultural Alignment, Emotional Dignity

THE ENABLED LIFE MODEL™

A good life is a **SAFE**, **FREE**, and **CONNECTED** life.

The Enabled Life Model™ is a foundation for human-centered living, built on three essential pillars that must work together. Imagine a **Three-Legged Stool**: Safety, Freedom, and Connection are the three legs. If you take away even one leg, the stool collapses, leaving the person without the foundation they need to truly thrive.

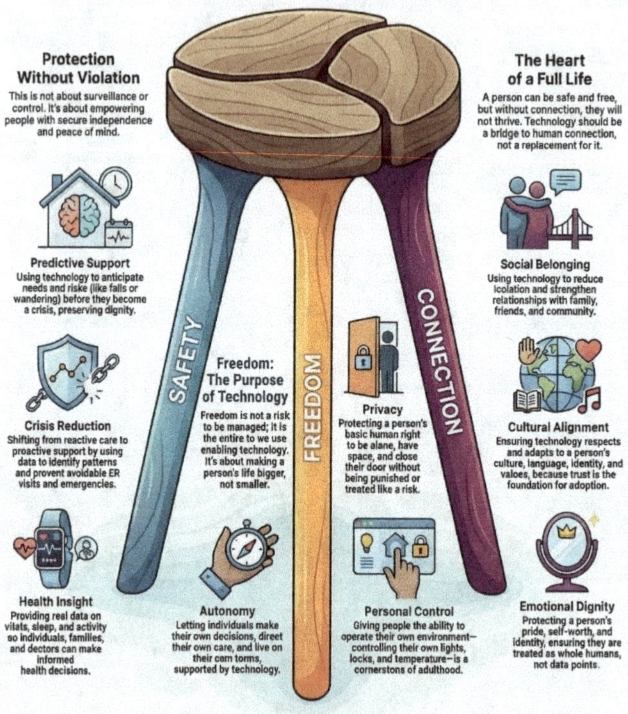

AN UNSTABLE FOUNDATION: WHEN A LEG IS MISSING

WITHOUT SAFETY:
A Life of Risk

Having freedom and connection without safety creates x precorious life. The stool is wobbly, and independence is fragile and unsustainable, constantly at risk of collapse.

WITHOUT FREEDOM:
A Life of Control

Having safety and connection without freedom feels like living in a gilded cage. It's secure but locks choice, privacy, and autonomy, stripping away dignity. The stool is rigid but traps the person.

WITHOUT CONNECTION:
A Life of Isolation

Having safety and freedom without connection results in an empty and lonely existence. The stool may be standing, but the person on it cannot thrive alone.

The Enabled Life Model™ as a Three-Legged Stool: What happens when a leg is missing

This is what care should be. This is what technology can do. This is what I am teaching the world.

FRAMEWORK 2: THE TECH EQUITY TRIANGLE™

The Ethical Foundation for Just, Human-Centered Technology

In Chapter 2, I introduced the Tech Equity Triangle™ as a systems-level framework. Let me go deeper here.

This framework is not about the individual. It's about the system. It's about states, funders, policymakers, technology vendors, provider associations, and anyone else who has the power to either open doors or keep them closed.

Because here's the truth: a person's Enabling Technology Ecosystem is dependent on the system doing its part first. If the system hasn't addressed access, if it hasn't redefined safety, if it hasn't committed to liberation, then the person is stuck. They can want remote supports all day long. Their team can build the most beautiful ecosystem plan you've ever seen. But if the infrastructure isn't there, if the policies don't allow it, if the funding doesn't support it, none of it matters.

The Tech Equity Triangle™ is the pusher. It's what keeps the movement moving.

The Structure

Visualize an equilateral triangle. At the center sits THE PERSON, their dignity, identity, history, and humanity. The three sides of the triangle represent the three conditions that must ALL be present for technology to be truly equitable: Access, Safety, and Liberation.

The Tech Equity Triangle™: A Blueprint for Systems Change — Access, Safety, Liberation with The Person at the center

When all three conditions are present, technology expands life. When even ONE is missing, technology becomes harmful.

ACCESS: Has the System Made This Possible?

Access is the foundation of equity. And access is not the person's responsibility. It's the system's responsibility.

Think about a state that wants to become a Tech First State. That sounds great on paper. They put enabling technology in the waiver. They talk about innovation. They encourage providers to explore remote supports. But if that state is largely rural, and most of its members live in areas with no reliable internet, no cell service, dead zones everywhere, then what have they accomplished? They've allowed something that their people can't actually use.

The Tech Equity Triangle™ says that's not good enough. Access means the system has to keep pushing. Work with cell phone service providers. Explore satellite options. Partner with internet companies to expand coverage. Don't just put technology in the waiver and walk away. Make sure your people can actually get to it.

Access also means affordability. If the technology exists but families can't afford it, that's not access. If the technology exists but it's not available in the languages your members speak, that's not access. If the technology exists but it's not designed for people who are Deaf, blind, or neurodivergent, that's not access.

Technology that only reaches some people is not innovation. It's modern segregation. And the Tech Equity Triangle™ holds systems accountable for closing those gaps.

SAFETY: Has the System Redefined What Safety Means?

Safety in traditional systems has been about control. Supervision. Monitoring. Compliance. But that definition of safety has caused harm, especially for communities that have historical reasons to distrust systems that claim to be watching out for them.

The Tech Equity Triangle™ demands that systems redefine safety. Safety is not control. Safety is protection that preserves dignity. And systems have to build that understanding into their policies, their procedures, their training, their oversight.

This means states and funders have to stop confusing surveillance with support. They have to create policies that allow for technology to be used in ways that are trauma-informed, culturally grounded, transparent, and consented to. They have to train their surveyors and auditors to understand the difference between monitoring that protects and monitoring that oppresses.

A camera in one home is support. A camera in another home is harm. Same device. Different meaning. Systems have to be sophisticated enough to understand that difference and create policies that honor it.

LIBERATION: Is the System Committed to Expanding Freedom?

Liberation is the soul of this framework. And it's the question that separates states that are truly Tech First from states that are just checking a box.

Liberation asks: Is this system actually committed to expanding freedom for the people it serves? Or is technology just being used to make the system more efficient, more comfortable, less liable?

Because technology can go either way. It can expand life or it can shrink it. It can give people more choices or it can give systems more control. The Tech Equity Triangle™ demands that systems commit to the expansion side. Technology should amplify freedom, not replace it.

This means funders have to stop only approving technology that benefits providers. It means states have to measure success not by how many devices are deployed, but by how many lives are expanded. It means policymakers have to ask: Are our people more free because of this technology? Do they have more choices? More dignity? More control over their own lives?

If the answer is no, the system hasn't met the standard of liberation.

When One Pillar Is Missing

The Tech Equity Triangle™ only works when all three pillars are present.

Access without safety becomes dangerous. You've opened the door, but you haven't protected the person walking through it.

Safety without liberation becomes oppressive. You've kept someone from harm, but you've also kept them from living.

Liberation without access becomes privilege. You've created freedom, but only for the people who could already get to it.

Access ensures people can begin. Safety ensures people can trust. Liberation ensures people can thrive.

Technology becomes equity when it increases access, protects dignity, and expands freedom, all at the same time. That's the standard. That's what the Tech Equity Triangle™ demands. And that's how I evaluate every piece of technology, every ecosystem, every decision.

FRAMEWORK 3: THE SEVEN FREEDOMS OF ET™

The Emotional and Human Model for Technology as Liberation

If the Enabled Life Model™ answers the what, and the Tech Equity Triangle™ answers the how, then the Seven Freedoms of ET™ answers the WHY.

Technology is not valuable because it's advanced. Technology is valuable because it returns freedom to people whose freedoms were taken by age, disability, trauma, inequity, fear, systems, outdated models, and lack of imagination.

The Seven Freedoms name the deep, emotional truths that people feel but rarely say out loud.

The Seven Freedoms of ET™: The seven core freedoms that technology must honor to move beyond outdated care models and restore dignity, choice, and liberation

Freedom 1: Safety Without Surveillance

The freedom to be safe without feeling watched, monitored, or infantilized.

Technology should protect, not control. Alert, not intrude. Support, not supervise. Safety should feel like dignity, not discipline.

This freedom addresses trauma, mistrust, racial profiling history, and institutional harm. For communities that have been watched, policed, and surveilled by systems that claimed to be helping, safety has to look different. It has to feel different.

Remember the young woman with the meta glasses? She wanted safety. She wanted support getting to her appointments, reminders to pick up her prescriptions. But she didn't want surveillance. She didn't want someone in the room reporting on her private conversation with her doctor.

When we found a way to provide the support without the surveillance, she went from non-compliant to 100% compliant. Because she was finally safe in a way that felt like dignity, not discipline.

When technology protects without intruding, when support is present but not oppressive, that is where freedom begins.

Freedom 2: Choice Without Constraint

The freedom to choose where to live, how to live, when to wake up, when to sleep, who enters your space, how you spend your time, what your day looks like.

Technology should expand choices, not shrink them.

In outdated systems, choice is treated as a privilege. Something you earn. Something that can be taken away. In an enabled life, choice is treated as a birthright.

Choice is the currency of independence.

Freedom 3: Privacy Without Punishment

The freedom to close your door, be alone, breathe without someone hovering, have boundaries, have space.

In traditional care models, privacy is treated like a risk. In my model, privacy is treated like a human right.

Technology gives privacy back safely through non-invasive sensors, door and environmental alerts, smart home tools, and supportive remote check-ins.

Privacy should never be punished. It should be protected.

Freedom 4: Independence Without Isolation

The freedom to live independently WITH connection built in.

People don't want to be alone. They want to be independent without being abandoned. Technology bridges this tension through remote supports, communication tools, accessible platforms, and smart home integration.

Independence becomes possible without fear of isolation. This freedom is essential for aging adults, for adults with disabilities, for people living alone, for families far away, for communities with staffing shortages.

Independence must come with connection, not loneliness.

Freedom 5: Identity Without Judgment

The freedom to be yourself without having to defend who you are.

Technology must affirm identity, not erase it. People deserve to be Black without assumptions. Deaf without exclusion. Autistic without being pathologized. Aging without dismissal. Multilingual without barriers. Culturally themselves without being misunderstood. Living with a disability without being treated like a child.

Identity is not a barrier. Identity is dignity. Enabling technology must respect identity, not erase it.

Freedom 6: Control Without Complexity

The freedom to control your environment, your routines, your home, your decisions, your sensory input, using technology that is intuitive, accessible, culturally aligned, easy to use, empowering, and responsive.

Control looks like setting your own lights, locking your own doors, adjusting your own temperature, communicating your own needs, managing your own space.

Control is adulthood. Control is safety. Control is self-definition.

Freedom 7: Joy Without Limitations

The freedom to experience joy, not just safety, not just stability, not just survival.

Joy is culture, music, food, community, identity, tradition, laughter, creativity, dancing, belonging. Joy is often ignored in care systems, as if the goal is simply to remain alive, not to feel alive.

But enabling technology opens doors to joy that systems have historically closed. Remember the young woman from Guatemala in Chapter 2? She used technology to reconnect with her culture, her language, her homeland. She regained her joy. Her identity. Her belonging.

Remember the woman with 100 questions? AI gave her the intellectual conversations she craved, the genius-level dialogue that no tired human could sustain. She got to experience the full depth of her mind. That's joy.

This is what technology can do when it's used with intention, dignity, and imagination. This is joy without limitations.

THE COMPLETE FRAMEWORK

The Seven Freedoms of ET™

1. Safety Without Surveillance

2. Choice Without Constraint

3. Privacy Without Punishment

4. Independence Without Isolation

5. Identity Without Judgment

6. Control Without Complexity

7. Joy Without Limitations

These freedoms are not theoretical. They are emotional truth. Cultural truth. Human truth. They are the freedoms every person deserves, and the freedoms enabling technology can restore when done with equity and humanity.

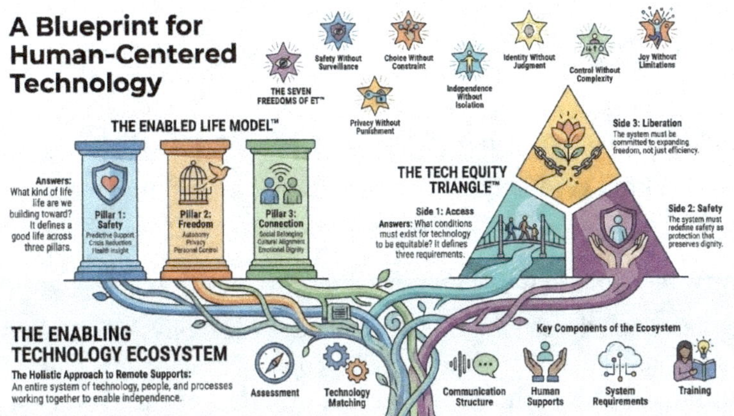

A Blueprint for Human-Centered Technology: The complete framework showing The Seven Freedoms of ET™, The Enabled Life Model™, The Tech Equity Triangle™, and The Enabling Technology Ecosystem working together

THE POSTURE REQUIRED: DREAM ENABLER VS. DREAM KILLER

Now let me tell you something that might be uncomfortable.

We are natural dream killers. Don't come at me. Don't come at me. But we are natural dream killers.

We are so quick to stomp on somebody else's dream because it's not something we would do, not something we care about, not something we have interest in. When we don't have those same interests, likes, dreams, desires, we will stomp all over somebody else's dream without even thinking about it.

I know this because I've lived it.

Most people who know me know I was severely obese and lost a significant amount of weight. More than 250 pounds. And I had tried to lose weight many times before. I would lose it, gain it back, plus some bonus points after that.

But I remember when I decided I was going to exercise every day for a year. Not just try, but commit. Every single day for a year. I needed to stop the insanity and do something different so I could get different results.

I grabbed a group of friends. We're going to do this together.

Child, did I not get all kinds of dream stompers in front of me.

"What do you want to do that for?"

"Why would you exercise every day?"

And then came the scientists. All of a sudden I had physical therapists. Occupational therapists. None of these people were actually any of these professions. But somehow they became experts when they wanted to stomp on my dream.

"Well, you know your body needs rest every…"

Who told you that? Where did you get that from? Who said that? What does that have to do with me saying I want to exercise every day? Did I say I was going to do super duper bodybuilding extreme fitness exercises every day? I never even got a chance to explain before all these instant professional clinicians showed up in my life.

When I decided I was going to do intermittent fasting, I never even got a chance to explain it.

"Well, you know you have to have three square meals a day."

"You know breakfast is the most important meal of the day."

All of a sudden everybody became a nutritionist and a dietician. Who told you that? If that's not your dream, don't stomp on mine. And I haven't even told you what kind of intermittent fasting I was going to do. Even if I did, it's not your dream to crush.

And we do this to people we support.

Let me give you an example that might seem extreme. But I tell extreme stories because I know you'll remember them.

Someone says, "Every Friday after I get paid, I want to buy a fifth of Bacardi. And I want to go to the strip club."

Now, what did you immediately think when I said that? What immediate stomping? Did you lace up your combat boots to stomp all over that dream? Or did you say, "What else? What's next?"

Your job, I don't care what your job description says, your job is to advocate. Not for what YOU want. For what THEY want.

How do I know that? Because there's a whole ISP. A whole plan of care. A whole person-centered process we go through to find out this person's wishes, dreams, wants, desires, outcomes, what works, what doesn't work. We go through a full process just to protect that. And we are supposed to be advocates of that person's life. Not what we feel.

Now, we are responsible for helping people make informed decisions. That's part of advocacy too. "Hey, you know if you drink a fifth of Bacardi every week, it could do some damage to your liver." I'm supposed to inform you of that.

And then if you say, "Okay, got it. Thank you very much, Precious. I still need to get to this liquor store and I need to go get my stack of ones."

It is not my job after that to say, "What do you want to go to a strip club for? Why does it have to be Bacardi?"

My job is to say, "Do you want it in a paper bag? And how many ones would you like to get from the bank?"

See, I'm a very spiritual person. The beautiful thing God gave us is the ability to rationalize and the ability to make a choice. Whether or not that's the right choice wasn't part of the equation. Because everything is permissible. It may not be beneficial. But these are the things we learn in life. This is what makes us who we are. This is how we learn.

I'm not doing that again.

There is a bottle of Southern Comfort somewhere in this world that will never see me again. You hear me? Because I learned that while that may have been permissible, it sure enough wasn't beneficial. I learned that because I was allowed to live it. And I lived it. Then I made a decision. That decision is mine and mine alone.

Because of that decision, the production of Southern Comfort has not stopped. But it's something that is now written into my personal plan of care. My personal ISP that says: Do not give Precious any Southern Comfort. Ever. Don't even let her smell it or see it. There will be an adverse response in her behavior if you do so.

This is what I want you to walk away with.

In order to be a dream enabler, you must first understand how you are a dream limiter. You must first see your own combat boots before you can take them off.

These frameworks I've given you, The Enabled Life Model™, The Tech Equity Triangle™, The Seven Freedoms of ET™, they only work if you have the right posture. If you're a dream killer, the frameworks won't save you. You'll find ways to use them to limit people.

But if you're a dream enabler, these frameworks become the most powerful tools you've ever had. They give you language. They give you structure. They give you permission to push back on systems that want to limit people. They give you a way to say, "No, this is what dignity looks like. This is what freedom looks like. This is what an enabled life looks like."

I want you to leave this chapter thinking: What's next? What else can we do? How more can I support? How more can I aid somebody living their best life?

If we're going to get charged with aiding and abetting, please let it be somebody living their best life.

Don't kill nobody else's dream. Don't stomp just because you wouldn't do it. That doesn't mean they wouldn't. That's the beautiful thing about being a human being.

Technology is moving too fast for us to keep going back. The further back we have to go to get people, the much farther it is to get back to the front. Because technology is not stopping.

Neither should we.

CLOSING: WHY THESE FRAMEWORKS MATTER

Let me tell you what these frameworks do.

For providers: They give you a way to assess whether your technology is actually serving people, or just serving compliance.

For policymakers: They give you language to write into waivers, regulations, and guidance.

For families: They give you a vocabulary to advocate for what your loved one deserves.

For people receiving support: They give you permission to demand more than survival.

For the field: They give us a shared foundation to build on.

These frameworks didn't come from a textbook. They came from 38 years of doing the work. From standing in homes. From sitting in ISP meetings. From fighting with systems. From advocating for people who were told no. From watching technology change lives. From learning what works and what doesn't.

These frameworks are my gift to the field.

Use them. Cite them. Build on them. Teach them. Challenge them. Improve them.

Because the future of care depends on us getting this right.

For training, keynotes, and consultation on these frameworks:

Precious "Preciosa" Myers-Brown

Chief Innovation and Dream Officer

Vista Supports, LLC

The Voice of Enabling Technology™

CHAPTER 6: THE POWER OF SMART SUPPORTS IN INDEPENDENCE

Why Technology Doesn't Replace People: It Releases Them

There's a long-standing misconception in our field that independence means less support, fewer people, or no staff involvement. But independence is not the absence of support. Independence is the presence of the right support.

People don't want to be left alone. They want to be empowered. They want control, dignity, privacy, safety, choice, and autonomy. Traditional systems taught us to equate independence with staff reduction. But true independence is person-driven, not staff-driven.

Enabling technology doesn't eliminate support. It reshapes support so people can live the life they want, with the support they choose.

The Shift: From Supervision to Supported Autonomy

For decades, the dominant belief in disability and aging services was simple: someone must always be present. This assumption didn't come from community living. It came from institutions.

Community life requires a different approach. Supported autonomy shifts us from constant observation to intelligent support, from supervision to connection, from caretaking to partnership, from control to collaboration, from intrusion to empowerment.

Smart supports give people privacy without risk, independence without fear, choice without penalty, and connection without surveillance. This is what community living was supposed to be. This is what it can finally become.

The Truth About Regulations That Nobody Talks About

Before I tell you the story that changed everything for me, I need to tell you something about regulations that most people in this field don't understand.

Regulations tell you WHAT outcomes you need. They hardly ever tell you HOW to do it.

Read that again.

The regulations give you the outcomes. They tell you what needs to be accomplished. But how you accomplish it? That's assumed. That's interpreted. That's where providers fill in the blanks based on how they THINK the regulation should be implemented.

But when you go back to the bare written word of the regulations, they rarely tell you how to do it. Which means innovation is built into the regulations whether people want to accept that or not. The framework allows for creativity. The framework allows for new approaches. The framework allows for technology.

Most providers don't see it that way. They've been operating the same way for so long that they think the way they do things IS the regulation. But it's not. It's just one interpretation. And there are other interpretations that could help people live better lives if we had the courage to try them.

That's what I learned in 2006.

STORY: The Man Who Wouldn't Open the Door (2006)

Let me take you back to 2006, years before "remote supports" was a phrase anyone in this field used.

I was supporting a man who received periodic supportive living services through a home and community-based waiver. On paper, staff were supposed to visit his home regularly to assist with tasks in his Individual

Support Plan, including medication administration.

But there was a problem.

He wouldn't open the door.

Not sometimes. Almost never.

Staff would show up. Knock. Wait. Nothing. They'd document "unable to make contact" and leave. The system labeled him "noncompliant." People whispered that he wasn't "engaging with the program." Some suggested we needed a behavior support plan. A psychiatrist. A team meeting to figure out why he was being so difficult.

But here's what I noticed:

He called me all day long.

All. Day. Long.

He'd call to talk about his day. He'd ask for help figuring something out. He'd want to go over his schedule. He'd share what was on his mind. He wanted connection. He wanted support.

He just didn't want people trekking through his house with their boots on. He didn't want to smell their cologne. He didn't want someone standing over him while he took his pills.

He was communicating something the system refused to hear:

"I want your support. I just don't want you in my space."

See, most of us learned to assert ourselves when we were two or three years old, telling our parents "No, I can do it myself!" That's how we developed autonomy, personality, preferences. People got into formation around who we were becoming.

But in the IDD system, many people are born into environments where someone is always there telling them what to do and when to do it. So when they push back, when they assert themselves, the system calls it "behavior." The system calls it a problem. The system calls in the professionals to fix them.

I called it something else.

I called it communication.

And I decided to listen.

My husband is a pediatric oncology nurse. One day he mentioned that the hospital had medication dispensing devices that gave kids more autonomy in taking their meds, instead of forcing a sick child to open their mouth on command.

I said, "Tell me more."

He explained how the device worked.

I said, "I need that."

He told me it was only for hospital use. Only for institutional settings. Not available for home and community-based services. No consumer version existed. No Google search would help me. This wasn't even a product you could buy.

I didn't care.

I called the manufacturer. I called every number I could find. I got transferred. I got dead ends. I kept calling.

Finally, I reached a woman who listened.

I told her what I was trying to do, without sharing any protected information. I told her about this man who wanted support but needed it delivered differently. I told her I believed innovation was our responsibility, not our option.

She said, "The device costs several hundred dollars, but I can give you a promotional demo price. We can't connect you to any system because there's no system for this. And I can't help you set it up. But I'll tell you how."

I said, "Whatever it takes."

I paid for it out of my own pocket. $300.

The agency I worked for wasn't trying to hear anything I was talking about. They weren't interested in innovation. They weren't willing to take the risk.

But I believed, and still believe, that it is our responsibility to listen beyond the disability, beyond the "behavior," beyond the label, to what the person is actually trying to experience.

So I bought the device. I brought it to him. I explained what it could do.

He said, "Yeah, let's give it a go."

The device was designed for hospital infrastructure, internal networks, nursing stations, institutional systems. We had none of that.

So we jailbroke it.

We hooked it to his phone system. When he took his medication, the device registered it. When he didn't, it called the nursing line, which we routed to our team.

First day, my phone rang.

It was him.

"Did you see? I took my meds!"

I could hear the pride in his voice. The excitement. The dignity.

"Yeah," I said. "We saw. You did great."

"This is great. This is fantastic!"

For the first time, we could prove he was receiving his medication, something we could never prove before because he never opened the door. For the first time, he had autonomy AND support. For the first time, the system worked FOR him instead of against him.

And do you know what happened next?

I caught all kind of heck.

The agency was upset because I wasn't "physically inside the house." The oversight people questioned the approach. People who had been perfectly fine NOT knowing whether he took his meds suddenly had a problem with me PROVING that he did.

But here's what I knew:

The goal was never to stand in his living room.

The goal was to help him live his best life. Meet his ISP outcomes. Maintain his health and safety. And teach him to eventually not need us at all.

That's what person-centered care actually means.

That's what enabling technology actually does.

And that moment, standing in my kitchen, phone in hand, hearing a man's joy because he finally got to do something HIS way, that was the moment I knew this was bigger than one person.

This was the future.

I just had to fight like hell to build it.

What Smart Supports Actually Are

Smart supports are often misunderstood. People hear "technology" and they think cameras watching people, automated staff replacement, digital versions of institutional control, or shortcuts for care.

That's not what smart supports are.

Smart supports are tools that reduce unnecessary intrusion while enhancing safety. They protect dignity while strengthening independence. They empower staff to work smarter, not just harder. They improve decision-making by providing truth instead of guesswork.

Smart supports don't watch people. They watch the environment. They detect patterns, changes, medical indicators, sleep disruptions, wandering events, and early signals of crisis, all with dignity intact. This is respectful support.

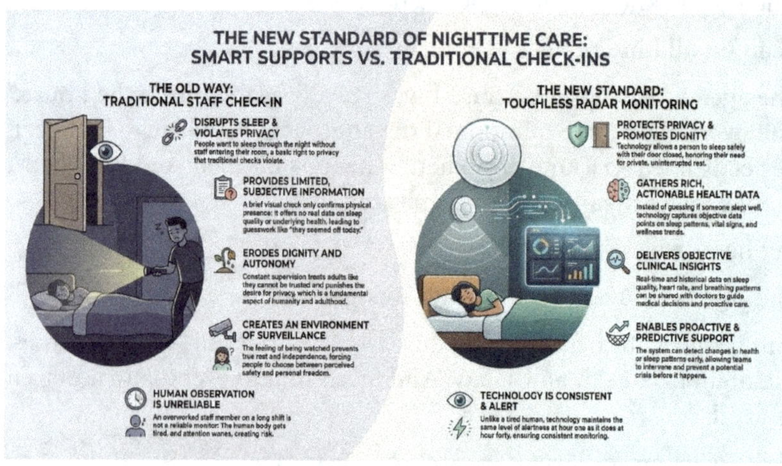

The New Standard of Nighttime Care: Smart Supports vs. Traditional Check-Ins — How technology protects privacy, promotes dignity, and delivers actionable health data

STORY: Independence Protected Through Intelligent Support

I once supported a man who lived alone, used a walker, and relied on portable oxygen. As his COPD worsened, he became concerned. But not about losing his independence. He was concerned about what might happen if something medical occurred when he was alone.

He wasn't asking for staff to live with him. He wasn't asking for a group home. He wasn't asking for around-the-clock supervision.

He was asking: "Are there options that let me stay independent and sleep with peace of mind?"

The staff around him dismissed the concern. "He doesn't need technology," they said.

My response was simple: "If he collapses or loses consciousness, how is he supposed to call you?"

Their silence said it all.

So we advocated. We pushed. And we implemented enabling technology: a sensor system that detected changes in his body, alert notifications to remote support, a backup responder who lived nearby, and intelligent monitoring that didn't invade his privacy.

Three weeks later, it happened.

He had a medical emergency in his sleep. Not a seizure like we originally suspected. A stroke. He didn't feel it. Didn't know it. Couldn't call. Couldn't move.

But the technology picked it up. It alerted remote support. A responder arrived. EMS was called.

He survived.

And because of that intervention, he continued living independently.

Smart supports didn't save his life. But smart supports saved his freedom long enough for people to save his life.

This is independence protected by intelligence, not supervision.

Smart Supports Are Staff Liberation, Not Staff Replacement

For decades, providers operated under rigid, outdated regulations that forced them to place staff where staff were not actually needed. Not because it was meaningful. Not because it reflected the person's needs. Not because it supported autonomy. But because the regs said so, or at least because that's how people interpreted the regs.

This led to wasted staff time, frustrated employees, overstaffed homes, understaffed emergencies, burnout, stagnant professional growth, and misuse of human talent. When you force people to occupy shifts instead of serve with purpose, you lose them. Not just physically. You lose their passion, their creativity, their commitment.

Enabling technology changes everything.

With tech-first, hybrid enabling technology environments, staff no longer just occupy shifts. They serve with purpose. They can be deployed strategically, work where they make the biggest impact, respond to real needs instead of imagined ones, and provide meaningful support instead of passive supervision.

This improves morale, retention, professional identity, career satisfaction, agency flexibility, person-centered practice, and financial sustainability. Agencies gain margin, savings, the ability to give raises, the ability to expand programs, and the ability to innovate. DSPs gain dignity, purpose, clarity, impact, and real professional expression.

This is the truth I keep coming back to: technology doesn't replace support. Technology gives you MORE support. More data. More context. More accuracy. More clarity. More insight. More predictability.

Staff are no longer guessing. Staff are no longer babysitting. Staff are no longer sitting in living rooms for eight hours because the regs require it. They are professionals again.

That is what liberation looks like for the workforce.

Smart Supports Improve Clinical Judgment

Smart supports don't just empower staff. They empower clinicians.

Before enabling technology, teams relied on staff memory, inconsistent reporting, approximations, subjective observations, and guesses. This is dangerous for people who are non-verbal, people with limited communication, elders living with dementia, people with intellectual disabilities, people with cognitive changes, and anyone unable to express their needs clearly.

Smart supports provide real data: sleep patterns, movement patterns, safety events, early warning indicators, baseline shifts, and objective information. This transforms ISP meetings, behavior support planning, clinical treatment, medication management, hospital visits, and emergency response.

Doctors can finally make decisions based on truth, not speculation. DSPs can provide insight based on data, not guesswork. Families experience peace, not uncertainty.

We're not guessing anymore. We're using quality data to guide judgment. This is what modern clinical care looks like.

Independence Is a Human Right, Not a Risk

Older systems feared independence. New systems honor it.

Independence is not reckless, dangerous, or irresponsible. Independence is developmental. It's how we grow. It's cultural. It's connected to our identity, our community, our history. It's psychological. We need autonomy to thrive. It's emotional. We need to feel in control of our own lives. It's spiritual. Our sense of purpose is tied to our ability to make choices. And it's identity-driven. Who we are is shaped by the decisions we make.

Smart supports protect independence without stripping away dignity, privacy, autonomy, control, culture, or belonging. This is independence WITH support. Independence WITHOUT intrusion. Independence WITH intelligence. Independence WITHOUT compromise.

This is the new model.

Closing: Smart Supports Make Care More Human

Smart supports do not make care less human. They make care more human.

They center autonomy. They reinforce dignity. They respect privacy. They empower staff. They improve clinical accuracy. They provide families peace. They modernize care models. They strengthen independence.

Smart supports don't shrink a person's life. They expand it. They don't remove support. They reorganize support around what actually matters.

This is the future of independence. This is the promise of enabling technology. This is the transformation the field has been waiting for.

Consent, Privacy & Data Governance: The Ethical Foundation

No conversation about enabling technology is complete without addressing the ethical framework that must govern its use.

Technology is a tool. Like any tool, it can be used for liberation or for control. The difference is consent, transparency, and clear governance.

The Consent Principle

No technology should ever be deployed without the informed, ongoing consent of the person it supports.

This means the person, or their legal representative, understands what the technology does. They understand what data is collected. They understand who has access to that data. They have the right to refuse or discontinue at any time. And consent is documented and revisited regularly.

Consent is not a one-time signature. It's an ongoing conversation.

The Privacy Protocol

Privacy is a right, not a privilege to be earned.

Clear protocols must define what is monitored versus what is not. Environmental sensors like motion and temperature are different from cameras. Most enabling technology does not require visual surveillance.

Protocols must define who has access. Only authorized personnel should see alerts and data, and access should be role-based and auditable. They must define how long data is retained, with clear policies that are limited and compliant with applicable regulations. They must define what triggers human intervention, because not every alert requires a response. And they must include "no camera" options, because many people can be safely supported with sensors alone. Visual monitoring should only be used when clinically necessary and with explicit consent.

The Data Governance Framework

Data collected through enabling technology belongs to the person it describes. Governance must include transparency, so people know what data exists about them. It must include access, so people or their representatives can review their own data. It must include security, with data encrypted and protected from unauthorized access. It must include minimization, so only necessary data is collected. And it must include audit trails, so all data access is logged and reviewable.

Avoiding Digital Institutionalization

Here's the fear we must name: that enabling technology could become a new form of institutionalization. Constant surveillance dressed up as support.

This is a real risk if we don't build ethical guardrails.

The test is simple: Does this technology make the person's life bigger or smaller?

If technology increases oversight without benefit, surveillance without consent, data collection without purpose, or restriction without safety justification, then it is not enabling technology. It is control technology.

Enabling technology expands life. Control technology shrinks it.

Every implementation should be measured against this standard.

CHAPTER 7: THE FUTURE WORKFORCE: STAFF, RETENTION & TECH-ENABLED SUPPORT

Why Technology Makes the Workforce Stronger, Safer, and More Sustainable

Let me tell the truth about the workforce crisis.

There is a workforce crisis. Not a staffing shortage. A workforce crisis. And we have to stop acting like a job fair, a bonus check, a pizza day, a new recruiting ad, or a "thank you" email will fix a crisis that is structural.

DSPs are underpaid, under-respected, overworked, under-supported, burned out, emotionally exhausted, spiritually depleted, carrying too much, and holding too many roles. The crisis didn't begin with COVID, but COVID exposed everything the field tried to hide.

DSPs show up with love, commitment, and resilience. But the truth is we cannot build the future of care on the backs of an exhausted workforce.

And the good news? We don't have to.

Enabling technology doesn't push DSPs out. It lifts them up.

The Reality of 48-Hour Shifts

Let me tell you what's really happening out there.

Forty-eight hour shifts are reality. It's sad to say, but because we are obligated to meet staffing ratios under the traditional model, when someone doesn't show up, you're stuck. There's no other option for providing that supervision. So before utilizing enabling technology to fill in the gaps, staff just got stuck.

When I was a DSP, I can't count how many times I got stuck on shift. After having already worked 12 hours, then 18 hours, then I get stuck on an overnight for another 12 hours, and then that shift is short too. So I'm still stuck there. I have worked 48-hour shifts. I have worked 72-hour shifts. And I was not my best self.

This is more common than we would probably want to admit. Providers, house managers, supervisors are at times at wit's end trying to figure out how to cover a shift. And we try to force ourselves, square peg into round hole. We try to force things to work.

But here's the truth: what you wind up having is bodies in a house.

If I've been working a 48-hour shift, how good is my body in that house? Yes, I may be present, but I'm not going to be on point. As much as I want to be, I may not be on point.

This is the same dilemma you see in industries that rely on people being very focused. Police officers, firefighters, EMS, nurses, doctors. I don't want that tired doctor. I don't want him operating on my body. As good as he may want to be, he's going to fall short. And I don't want to be the patient that he falls short on.

You see in hospitals, maybe they have the sleeping beds for the doctors. But I haven't seen any sleeping beds for nurses. And nurses work longer shifts and more shifts than even the doctors. But I also don't want a sleepy nurse. I want people who are fresh.

And here's the thing that's so interesting: even the hospitals in an acute care setting are using technology to fill those gaps. If the nurse misses something or is on their rounds dealing with another patient, the machine tells you when somebody needs extra support, when they need the call or code. The machines, the technology, fill in the gap.

So if the most acute care settings, which is our hospitals, rely on technology, why is it that we have a problem doing it for people who are not in an acute situation? Yes, they need support. Yes, they may need oversight. Yes, they may need assistance. But they also could utilize our remote assistance as well.

This is not an argument. We need to find a way to bring innovative solutions to a very traditional field.

Why DSPs Are Leaving (and It's Not What You Think)

DSPs don't leave because they don't care. They leave because the system makes it impossible to stay.

They feel invisible. The work is harder than the pay. Expectations are unrealistic. The emotional load is overwhelming. Staffing ratios are unfair. Everything is a crisis. Nothing is predictable. Regulations were written for institutions, not homes. They don't feel safe. Burnout becomes survival. And there is no path forward.

But here's what really makes them leave: they are afraid of being blamed.

In many states and jurisdictions, the regulatory mindset operates under something called a Protection From Harm framework. In theory, it's supposed to protect people with disabilities. But in practice? It often becomes a system of automatic blame.

Here's how it plays out.

Let's say you have four people with IDD living in a home and two staff on shift. Now imagine a typical situation: one person needs to be showered, so one staff goes to the bathroom. Another person needs help using the restroom or with a Hoyer lift, so the second staff goes to the other bathroom. The remaining two housemates are sitting safely in the living room watching TV.

Everything is fine. Everyone is cared for. Everyone is within staffing ratios.

Then it happens. One person in the living room gets up, walks into the kitchen, and unexpectedly falls.

This is where the system shows its cracks.

Even if staff were doing exactly what they were supposed to do, even if everyone was within regulatory ratios, even if it was physically impossible to be in three places at once, even if the fall was nobody's fault, the Protection From Harm framework often requires an incident investigation, immediate staff removal from the home, and investigative leave without pay.

Without pay.

And nobody can tell them how long the investigation will take. They can't work anywhere else during the investigation. Their life stops. Their bills don't.

I have seen staff on investigative leave for months. Months. That's ridiculous. Sometimes it's warranted, but the majority of times it's not. And when you think about everything I've been talking about in this book, sometimes it's our own system that puts that staff person in a predicament where it was impossible for them to be five places at one time.

It is impossible. I don't care what the regulations say. You cannot provide continuous active treatment to six people with two staff on duty. Yes, we may say okay, hold this puzzle piece while I go help somebody eat or help somebody bathe. But just because they are holding a puzzle piece doesn't mean they're receiving continuous active treatment. That's the setup. That's how staff end up in impossible situations.

And when something happens? Two people doing their best within an impossible system are now treated as if they committed neglect. This happens every day.

DSPs know this. DSPs feel this. DSPs fear this. This is why some staff avoid certain homes. This is why some hide mistakes. This is why some leave the field entirely. Because they know one incident, even an unavoidable one, could jeopardize their livelihood.

Technology Protects the Workforce

This is where enabling technology becomes revolutionary.

When I implement hybrid enabling technology environments, remote sensors, remote supports, two-way audio and video, safety alerts, I'm not replacing staff. I'm protecting staff.

With smart supports, DSPs can safely assist in the bathroom while remote support monitors the living room, while sensors watch for environmental risk, while alerts track movement, while DSPs feel protected by an additional presence. And if something does happen, clinicians can later see the real sequence of events.

This is the support staff deserve. This is safety. This is partnership. This is accountability that does not punish people for doing their job.

Technology becomes the second set of eyes, the backup brain, the safety partner, the truth teller, the protector of DSPs who are doing everything right.

No more staff being punished for impossible situations. No more being afraid to go to work. No more investigative leave for being human.

Technology does not just support the people receiving services. Technology protects the people giving the services. That's why DSPs feel more secure with smart supports, why quality DSPs stay when tech is present, and why providers need enabling technology to stabilize their workforce.

The Story Nobody Wants to Tell: When Staff Resist Technology

Now, I want to be clear. Most DSPs welcome technology. They're tired. They want help. They want to feel supported and protected.

But not everyone.

I supported a woman who used a wheelchair and had paralysis on one side. She wanted independence. She wanted to see who was at her door, decide when to open it, and control her home environment.

So we installed a Ring doorbell system. Not for surveillance, but to give her autonomy. The house manager also received notifications as a backup safety plan.

Then the truth surfaced.

One DSP had been consistently arriving late to their shift. The Ring doorbell exposed it. Not through spying, but through honesty.

Instead of adjusting their behavior, the DSP sabotaged the technology. Cut the wires. Over and over.

This wasn't fear of innovation. It was fear of accountability.

And this is the deeper truth: technology didn't replace staff. Technology revealed the misuse of staff. It showed who was actually doing their job, who needed support or retraining, where staffing adjustments were needed, and where systems were failing people.

DSPs don't fear technology. They fear unfair systems. And the staff who do fear technology? Sometimes it's because technology tells the truth they've been hiding.

This story proves why the workforce model must evolve.

The Turnover Trauma Nobody Talks About

I talk a lot about DSPs, but I also want to talk about the turnover trauma this causes for the people we support.

Let's imagine if you needed total care. Every person that turns over is a new person that has to learn your body. A new person that has to be taught how to shower you, how to bathe you, how to touch you, how to feed you.

That is traumatic. Just the thought of it alone is traumatic.

I'm a person that has had the same doctors for two decades at least. I can't even imagine. Let me tell you something. If my doctor is sick, guess what? I'm rescheduling the appointment. You know why? Because I don't feel like having to reorient a new doctor to me, my body, my problems, and my history. I will reschedule.

You may think, well Precious, that's irresponsible. I don't care. I have the authority. I have the right. I have the privilege of being able to do so.

The people we work with don't have that privilege. They just have to accept it and take it. New person, new body, new everything. And that new person coming in is learning from probably somebody that's no longer there.

Yes, we train to the ISP. We train to the plan of care. We train to their records. But the records hardly ever have the nuances that people have learned about that person or for that person. There's conversations that a parent might have had with a staff person that they're carrying around as valuable gold knowledge to support that person. Maybe it never got written into the formal plan because there's no space on the formal plan for it. Or maybe somebody didn't share it. I don't know.

All I know is that there are AI systems that know more about us individually than the new staff would know about a person they needed to support. Because technology can remember things that humans can't or forget.

Technology can be trained to remember those nuances. To passively take in information so that when the next person comes on board, they can be reminded. They can ask the technology, how does this person like to be bathed? And the AI would remember what those things are.

Every one of us have little things we like about how we live our lives. So do the people we support. And it's important for somebody to feel good, to feel clean, to feel like they got their needs met. That's very subjective to that person. There's no universal way to approach somebody feeling good.

How many times has somebody we supported had to learn a new staff person? And how long, if ever, did it take for the new staff person to know how they like to be cared for? Things they learned that they liked along the way that maybe the previous staff person who no longer works there knew and carried that information away with them.

It is traumatic. And we talk a lot about trauma-informed care. Yet we seem to think that this is so easy for someone with a cognitive disability, a physical disability, to transition to turnover staff over and over again for their entire life. That's amazing that they deal with that. But how much more should we traumatize them when there's clearly technology that can remember that for them?

Even doctors are walking around dictating their notes so that they don't forget and so that it can be transferred to the next shift. Why are we acting like we don't know how this thing works?

Let's get it together.

The Future Workforce: Gen Z and Beyond

When you have these conditions where staff keep finding themselves on the side of getting in trouble, where they feel unsupported, it's very hard to recruit and encourage people into this field.

Listen, we all are only hoping and praying and wishing that we get to age well. And if we age well, we might need some support. What if there's nobody left to support us?

I'm Gen X. You best believe I'm making an investment in this, not just for the current people but for the future people, for all of us and the people behind us. But if we don't create solutions where people feel comfortable doing a job that supports them, why would they ever want to join this field?

And we're talking about Gen Z. Gen Z doesn't know anything but technology. Gen Z was born into a 100% technology world. Do you think they would want to be in a field that has zero tech? They don't even understand what you're talking about.

But we can easily entice Gen Z to help us find ways to integrate technology, to utilize technology, even in ways we might not even think about today. Because they were born in it. They don't know anything but the use of technology in their lives. For them, it may be easier to come up with solutions.

We need to make sure we create space for that. I'm talking today and I'm talking future.

Closing: Technology Doesn't Replace the Workforce: It Finally Protects It

Technology doesn't eliminate the workforce. It strengthens it.

It gives DSPs dignity. It gives providers stability. It gives clinicians accuracy. It gives families peace. And it gives people supported the independence they deserve.

DSPs are superheroes. But they're also human. And we overwork them. Our field overworks whoever shows up to work. We have a workforce crisis, and truth be told, we always had a workforce crisis. But it's getting worse. You don't have a lot of people signing up voluntarily to do this type of work. So those who show up get overworked. And overworked means their patience grows thin. Even though they love what they do.

I know so many passionate, loving DSPs. People I would call with a drop of the dime if I needed help. But they can grow weary and tired too.

A mother's love is undefeated. A mother's love is almost superhuman when it comes to protecting her child. But even a mother can say, I need a break from these kids. They're getting on my nerves.

If a mother can say that, then a DSP, who is a superhero but still human, can feel the same way. And they deserve support. They deserve technology that fills the gaps. They deserve to not be punished for impossible situations. They deserve to feel safe at work.

This is the future of our workforce. This is the new model. And this is how we build a sustainable care system that honors everyone involved.

DSPs are not being replaced. They are being redefined. Their roles become higher-skilled, respected, modern, sustainable, and dignified. They are the backbone of this field, and technology simply builds muscle around that backbone.

DSPs are essential. They are the future. And technology is finally giving them the support they've always deserved.

CHAPTER 8: AGING IN PLACE: FREEDOM, DIGNITY, AND THE FUTURE WE'RE BUILDING FOR OURSELVES

What Aging in Place Really Means

Let me tell you what aging in place really means.

It's not about staying in a house. It's about staying in a life.

It's about waking up in a bed that smells like you. Cooking breakfast on a stove you know how to operate without thinking. Sitting in the chair that's molded to your body from years of use. Looking out the window at a view you've watched change with the seasons.

It's about the sound of your neighborhood. The kids playing, the dog barking, the ice cream truck in summer.

It's about knowing which floorboard creaks. Which cabinet sticks. Which light switch needs two tries.

It's about a life you built, in a space that holds your memories, surrounded by routines that give you comfort.

Home means security. It means a foundation. It means an opportunity to do things you might not do outside. We all do things in our house that we wouldn't do anywhere else. Maybe you do a funny dance in front of the mirror. Maybe you walk around in your underwear because you're in your home and you feel secure in that. Home is where you can just sit and look at the wall if that's what you want to do. Where nobody is talking in your ear. Where nobody is asking you, are you ready to take your meds? Are you ready to go to bed? Do you have to go to the bathroom? Are you ready to go to day program?

That can be annoying. And I appreciate my alone time. I'm sure everyone appreciates alone time.

But I have known people who have never had a moment alone since the day they were born. They've always had somebody in their face. Can you imagine how awful that might be? If you had somebody in your face 24/7?

Aging in place is about freedom. The freedom to live and die on your own terms, in a place that feels like yours.

And if that place happens to be an assisted living facility or a retirement community where you chose to go because you're tired of mowing the lawn and cooking every night? That's freedom too. Because aging in place isn't about the physical location. It's about choice. It's about having options. It's about being trusted to decide what's best for your own life.

The Two Populations We're Not Talking About

When most people think about aging in place, they think about seniors. Grandma who wants to stay in her house. Grandpa who refuses to leave the home he built with his own hands.

And that's valid.

But there's another population that's aging, one that the system has almost completely ignored in the aging-in-place conversation: people with intellectual and developmental disabilities.

People with IDD are living longer than ever before. In the 1970s, the average life expectancy for someone with Down syndrome was 25 years. Today? It's 60+ years. People with cerebral palsy, autism, and other developmental disabilities are aging into their 60s, 70s, and 80s. They are becoming dual-diagnosis: aging adults with lifelong disabilities.

And the system has no idea what to do with them.

Here's the typical scenario. A person with IDD lives in a supportive living residence, a group home, or an ICF for decades. They have a community they know, staff who understand them, a routine that works, friends they've made, a life they've built.

Then they develop age-related medical conditions. Diabetes. Heart disease. Mobility limitations. Dementia or cognitive decline. Increased medical complexity.

And suddenly, the system says: "We can't support you here anymore.

You need to go to a nursing home."

The Problem with Nursing Homes for People with IDD

Nursing homes are equipped for medical care. They are not equipped for people with lifelong cognitive disabilities.

There's a massive difference between someone who had full cognitive function for 70 years and then developed dementia, and someone who has had a cognitive disability their entire life and is now also aging.

One is experiencing cognitive loss. The other has been navigating cognitive differences for decades and has developed a lifetime of adaptive strategies.

These are not the same. But nursing homes treat them the same.

The staffing ratios alone tell the story. In many ICF or supportive living environments, the staffing ratio might be 1 staff to 2 people, or 1 staff to 4 people. In a nursing home, the ratio is often 1 CNA to 15 or even 30 residents. That's a massive reduction in individualized support.

And nursing homes are built for dealing with medical care, whereas home and community-based waiver services and ICFs are built with habilitation in nature, dealing with the cognitive disabilities. People are trained around that, not just the medical. It's a very specialized service.

When a person with IDD enters a nursing home, they often lose their specialized support because most nursing home staff are not trained in IDD. They don't understand how this person communicates, what behaviors mean, what triggers distress, what brings comfort, or how to support developmental needs alongside medical needs.

They lose their community. The friends they made. The staff who knew them. The routines that gave them stability. The life they built.

They lose their identity. In a supportive living home, they were Michael or Sarah. In a nursing home, they become the patient in Room 12.

And for someone who has relied on specialized, person-centered care their entire life, that reduction can be devastating.

STORY: Home Isn't Just a Place, It's Hope

Let me tell you about a man I supported.

He had lived in his home for 30 to 40 years. Not a family home. His own home. The place he had made his. The routines he had built. The community he belonged to.

Then his health declined.

He needed surgery. The surgery went okay, but recovery was harder than expected. He declined a bit, recovered a bit, but ultimately needed to go to a step-down facility for rehab.

We thought it would be temporary. Maybe four weeks. It became eight weeks. Then sixteen weeks. Then months.

His home didn't have the level of nursing support he needed during recovery. We tried to get temporary funding for additional nursing services in his home. The request was denied. So he stayed in the nursing facility.

And that's when everything started to fall apart.

He started to get depressed. Not because his medical condition was worsening. But because he wasn't home.

He wasn't in an environment he recognized. He wasn't around people who knew him. He wasn't eating his favorite foods. He wasn't sitting in his favorite chair at the dining room table. He wasn't going outside to the spot where he liked to sit. He wasn't talking to the neighbors he'd known for years.

All of that was gone.

And while he needed to recover medically, he was losing something far more important: his will to live.

He started to refuse to talk. He refused to eat. He refused to bathe. He refused to go to the bathroom and started urinating on himself, even though he was fully capable of using the toilet. He was shutting down.

The medical team saw a man who was declining. They thought his condition was getting worse, that he needed to stay longer, that he wasn't ready to go home, that maybe he'd never be ready.

But that wasn't the truth. The truth was he was depressed. He was grieving. He was giving up, not because he couldn't go home, but because he didn't believe he would go home.

A few of us went to visit him. Myself and two staff members. He wasn't responding. He wasn't answering us. He was looking at us, but he refused to speak. You could see in his eyes that he was listening, but he gave us no indication that he agreed with anything we were saying.

So I looked at him and said: "If you want to go home, I need you to get better. You have to get up. You have to start doing the things you know how to do."

He just stared. We stayed for a little while longer, then left. And after we left, he declined even more.

A few days later, the QIDP and the nurse from the organization went to visit him. When they got there, they found him walking around the hallway like the mayor, talking to everyone, smiling, engaged.

They were stunned. "What happened?!" they asked.

He looked at them and said: "Oh, I had a little talk with Jesus last night. And He told me I need to get it together. So I got it together. Now I'm ready to go home. What time y'all coming to pick me up?"

After two or three days of him consistently showing improvement, we finally had the discharge meeting. He went back home. And he was happy for years and years after that.

Not because the nursing facility was bad. Not because the staff weren't trying. But because home gave him hope. And hope gave him life.

STORY: When We Couldn't Get Her Home

Not every story ends that way.

For as long as I've been in the field, unanimously, anytime somebody goes to a nursing home or a facility that's not where they have familiar faces and familiar support, we try our best to get them back to their environment. Because we've seen too many times where people start to decline. Not because of substandard care. I'm not saying that. However, the staffing ratio in a residential habilitation or ICF is much better than in a nursing home. And people in our field are trained around the cognitive disabilities, not just the medical.

So anytime somebody has to go to a nursing home for recovery, whether it's a step-down unit or some kind of rehabilitation, we try our best. We visit. We go there. We talk to the staff. We send regular staff there so that they see familiar faces. We even do it when someone is hospitalized because we know about the benefits it has on people with cognitive disabilities.

But there was this one time with this young lady. She started to decline and needed to go to the hospital. Then from the hospital, she went to a nursing home. She had a terminal illness, and eventually she would need hospice.

It's not easy all the time to get everybody to agree that a person should have hospice in the home environment they've been living in for decades. I don't know why that is. But this person, she was so particular about her things. About the way her bedroom was. About where her pocketbooks were. About where the little trinkets sat.

And she was in that nursing home, and all she did was talk about the pocketbooks, the trinkets, and her bedroom. Because she was very particular about it. And she kept asking, when is she going home?

We didn't have an answer, but we were trying.

She was slowly declining. To the point that she eventually stopped believing us that we were trying to get her home. And then she kind of stopped talking.

We were trying our best to get her to have hospice in the home so that she would have closure, the staff would have closure, her housemates would have closure.

But she just declined even further. There's no amount of time that we could have sent people to stay with her 24/7 in that facility. The little bit of time we were able to send staff or be there was meaningful. But she just declined and declined and declined.

And then she expired while in a nursing home.

I remember that story because it upset me that I could not get her to feel her most comfortable in her final moments.

These are real things. These are real things that happen.

The Cultural Meaning of Home

Let me take you back to my grandmother for a moment.

She left Barnwell, South Carolina, left everything she knew, everyone she loved, to come to New York. She spent more years in New York than she ever spent in South Carolina.

But you know what she always called South Carolina? Home.

Even after decades in Harlem. Even after building a whole life in Queens. When she and my uncles would make their weekly trips down South to go to the Piggly Wiggly, clean off the property, visit family, she would always say: "We're going home."

Home isn't just a location. Home is where you come from. Home is where you belong. Home is where your story started, or where your chosen story lives.

For my grandmother, home was red soil and Barnwell and her mama's house and the community she was raised in.

For the man I supported, home was 30-40 years of mornings in his favorite chair, evenings on his porch, neighbors who waved when he walked by.

For the woman who couldn't come home, it was her pocketbooks and trinkets and the bedroom she had made hers.

Home is not a building. Home is a feeling. Home is dignity.

And aging in place is about protecting that dignity, no matter where home is.

STORY: "Can You Close My Door?"

Let me tell you about a moment that might not mean anything to anybody else. But for me, it meant everything.

We were building a smart home in DC, and we set up the residents to be able to control the temperature of their home, control the door, control the television, control the microwave, control a number of things with either automation or some device or some switch.

We had trained them, and they are super smart. But I remember one lady, she said, "It's cold."

So I told her, "If it's cold, you could control the temperature. Remember what we learned?"

And she looked at that iPad. Then looked back at me. Looked back at the iPad. Then looked back at me.

And she said, "I can control it?"

I said, "Yeah, that's what we've been doing all this time. You control your own home. You don't need me to change the temperature. Make it be whatever you want it to be."

And she was like, "Oh!" Like really in shock. "I get to do it?"

I said, "Yeah, you get to do it. Take control."

And she was like, "Oh my goodness."

We weren't even giving it back. We were giving it to her for the first time. And these are elderly seniors.

Then there was another young lady. She was controlling everything in her bedroom. Before, she used to leave the door open to her bedroom so that staff could hear her if she called out. That was just the protocol. So the staff would hear her when she needed something.

But we had set up some audio drop-ins so she could easily notify the staff when she needed something without leaving her door open.

We spent weeks practically living there with them to make sure they learned how to use that technology. And that they understood it was their home. And giving them back their power. Not even giving it back. Giving it to them for the first time.

For a lot of people, what happened next wouldn't mean anything. But for me, knowing them, knowing them when they needed my full support, and then watching them experience this level of independence and privacy? It means the world to me. I live for these moments. I look for these moments. And I work just so I could get more of these moments.

She was in her room showing us how she can control the TV, how she could control the blinds, how she could control the device on her bedside.

So we were like, "That's so good!"

And we were leaving out her room to go check on the other lady.

And she says, "Hey, can you close my door?"

That might not mean anything to anybody. But for me, it meant that she had the opportunity to have a private moment. And she knew it.

That's the difference. It's not like we close her door for her all the time. She knew that she had the power to have a private moment because she had technology that if she needed to call out to the staff, she could use that to notify them across the house or in the kitchen or wherever they were.

That's powerful. It does it for me.

Preparing the Future for Me

Now let me get personal with you.

I am Gen X.

For me, aging in place looks like a rebirth of mature youth. It looks like I done passed everything I needed to pass in life to arrive at this point to now live it fully. Without the pressure of having to be a teenager, be in the midst of building a career, learning how to be a new wife, dealing with the upsets of life. I have lived, and now I'm enjoying.

That's why I invest in my health. I used to be very unhealthy. And when I finally got it together, I always say there's nothing that feels better than feeling better. I feel good. And I want to maintain that.

But there are some things about aging that scare me.

I'm a dancer. I love to dance. I'm very active. I like to travel. I like to stay involved. I like to read. I like to keep using my mind. I don't want to just be a couch sitter. I want to stay active. I want to continue to dance for as long as I can. I want to continue to move my body.

I worked very hard on my weight loss and my health to regain it so that I can live with this body longer. I have the energy now. I didn't at one point. But now I do. So when I think about aging, I'm like, if this is good now, I just need it to get better. I don't want it to get worse. I want my mind to stay intact. So I stay learning and growing and doing things that keep my brain in function.

But sometimes when I think about aging, I think about who's going to be around.

I think about Susie from the story earlier in this book. When she left the sheltered workshop and left her large group home, how she felt isolated.

Will all my friends be around? Will I have new friends? Or will I be in a place that doesn't have a lot of relationships that I've had all my life?

That part is a little scary.

And when I think about those fears I have internally, I can appreciate what it's like for people with disabilities within these services. They have to deal with this all the time.

So what I'm attempting to do is try to secure a future that is better for today and better for the future. A future that I may not need right this second, but that I may need later. I'm trying to create a future that's ready for us.

Gen X is a different breed. We're at this point where we're thinking about retirement, and our retirement looks definitely different from the baby boomers. Definitely more active. More petty. But we want to be able to enjoy our golden years because we've been so serious for most of our lives.

I'm also thinking about my friends. Are they investing in their health? Where will we all live? I don't even know. But these are the kinds of things I think about as I start to do my planning and think about what the future looks like.

Has the future been prepared for me?

Because I don't want to age in a 1988 system. I don't want to age in a nursing home where staff don't know my name, my story, my preferences. I don't want to age in a place that strips me of my autonomy, my privacy, my choices.

I want to age in the world I'm helping to build right now.

And if I want that for myself, I better make damn sure I'm building it for everyone else.

Because the future I'm preparing isn't just for them. It's for me. It's for you. It's for all of us.

Tech Equity and Aging in Place

Here's the truth: aging in place without technology is a luxury only the wealthy can afford.

If you have money, you can hire private caregivers, install smart home systems, pay for 24/7 monitoring, and access concierge medical care.

If you don't have money, you get whatever Medicaid will cover, whatever staff are available if any, whatever the system says you "qualify" for. And usually, that means a nursing home.

That's not equity.

Tech equity means everyone, regardless of income, disability, race, language, or location, has access to the technology that lets them age safely in the place they call home.

Tech equity means a single mother with MS can stay in her apartment with her kids because remote monitoring and smart home devices give her the support she needs. A man with autism can age in his group home because technology supplements the nursing care he requires. A grandmother in a rural community can stay on her family's land because telehealth and sensors keep her connected and safe.

This is what we're building. This is what's possible. This is the future we deserve.

Closing: We Build the Future Now

Let me bring this full circle.

My grandmother left Barnwell, South Carolina, to pursue a dream. A dream of having more options, more choices, more freedom than the segregated South would allow her.

She didn't know exactly what that dream would look like. She just knew she had to build it.

And now, decades later, I'm writing a book about building homes and options and freedom for people the system has forgotten.

She laid the foundation. I'm continuing the work.

And now I'm asking you to join me.

Because aging in place isn't just about seniors. It's not just about people with disabilities. It's about all of us.

It's about building a system that honors dignity, choice, culture, identity, independence, and connection.

It's about using technology not to replace humanity, but to protect it.

It's about ensuring that when we age, and we will, we have the options our grandparents never had.

We build the future now so we can age in it later.

That's not just policy. That's personal. That's legacy.

Let's build it together.

CHAPTER 9: WHEN SYSTEMS FAIL: THE HUMAN COST OF NOT INNOVATING

Why Outdated Models Hurt the People They Were Designed to Protect

Let me tell you what keeps me up at night.

It's not the technology. It's not the funding. It's not the politics.

It's the people who fall through the cracks of systems that were supposed to protect them.

Every day, across this country, people are placed in settings that don't fit them because "that's what's available." Staff are punished for situations they couldn't control. Families are told "we don't have the resources" while money flows to outdated models. Independence is denied because regulations can't imagine anything different. Lives are made smaller to fit into systems that refuse to grow.

These are system failures. Not failures of individuals. Not failures of effort. Not failures of caring. Failures of imagination. Failures of structure. Failures of will.

And until we name them, we can't fix them.

This chapter is about naming them.

System Failure #1: We Trust Strangers But Not Technology

Here's something that has always baffled me.

When I propose implementing enabling technology, sensors, remote monitoring, smart home devices, I hear: "I don't trust the technology." "What if it fails?" "That feels like surveillance." "People don't want to be monitored."

But let me ask you something.

Do you have any idea what actually happens inside a group home, a nursing facility, an ICF, or any residential setting?

If you're a manager, director, owner, or family member, do you really know what's happening when you're not there?

The truth is you don't.

You don't have cameras in every room. You don't have sensors tracking movement. You don't have data on what time staff arrived or left. You don't have records of every interaction.

You're trusting that it's happening the way it's supposed to happen.

You're trusting strangers. You're trusting that the person you hired is doing what they said they would. You're trusting that the training stuck. You're trusting that nobody is cutting corners.

And most of the time, that trust is warranted. Most DSPs are good people doing hard work.

But here's the irony: we trust complete strangers with the most intimate aspects of people's lives, bathing, toileting, medication, safety, but we say we "don't trust" technology that would actually provide data, accountability, and transparency.

Technology doesn't replace trust. Technology verifies trust.

Technology doesn't surveil people. Technology provides data that protects people.

When we refuse technology because we "don't trust it," we're actually choosing blind faith over informed care.

That's a system failure.

System Failure #2: We Silence the Voices We Claim to Empower

This one hurts my heart the most.

We spend all this time teaching people about self-advocacy. Teaching them about their rights. Teaching them about the opportunity to express their authentic self, to make choices, to be the author of their own life, to author their person-centered plan.

And yet. And yet.

I've seen too many times when a person is clearly articulating what they want, saying I want this, I want to live like this, I want to go over here, expressing it very well. But the system punishes them for having desires that are different from what the family thinks they should have or what others want them to decide.

Let me tell you about Bobby.

Bobby is a wheelchair user. He needs some physical assistance. But he is very capable. He's one of the most articulate self-advocates I know. He can express his wants, desires, interests, and needs. He can tell you how he wants things done and when he wants them done.

Bobby wants to live more independently with technology. He loves technology. He feels like he has outgrown his current environment and wants something more, like many of us have probably felt at some point in our lives. He wants to be able to utilize more technology and just call people when he needs them instead of having staff in his face all day.

But instead of everyone appreciating what he's saying, everyone turned to his family or his circle of support to question whether that would be the right decision.

And the last time I checked, we're supposed to help people make informed decisions, and then we're supposed to respect their choice. Dignity of risk. Person-centered planning. My life. No meeting about me without me. All these principles we claim to follow.

But somebody had a meeting on the side and decided they didn't want him to make that decision.

Bobby has no clue why his family is against him moving or living more independently. Probably their fear, because he needs some physical assistance. But those who are blocking him don't really know him. They're working from the memory of him when he needed more, or when he didn't self-advocate. They haven't had the chance to meet the new him.

I would describe Bobby as jovial. He's the life of the party. Super, super happy. He still calls me to this day. We still talk on the phone. He's a joy.

But he's unhappy. He's unhappy because he doesn't get to live where he wants to live, how he wants to live. And he just keeps saying, "Well, my family and them don't want me to live the way I want to live."

He's sad. He's actually saying those words.

And yet his circle of support, his team, the system, is failing him.

Here's what I always wonder: Bobby is a person who can articulate, who can express his wants and desires and what his anticipated outcomes are. What about the people who can't articulate like that?

And that's what I say about technology too. When someone can't articulate that their body is doing something funny on the inside, that's where technology can step in and advocate and speak on their behalf. But when we reject that, it's like we're rejecting the person from living their best life.

Just like Bobby. He is telling everybody who would listen what his best life looks like. But somehow the family's voice, other people's voices, are more important than the one he is using to express his own life.

We have to do better as a system. When somebody is able to articulate, we should be running to help support that voice. When someone is unable to articulate what's going on with their body, we should be advocating for technology to help them.

I can't even imagine what it's like to be experiencing something in your body and not be able to articulate it so you can get support. It must feel like suffocation. It must feel like drowning. Not being able to scream out, "Something's happening with my body, y'all. It's different."

But you don't know. And maybe you only do vital signs once a week or once a month. Who knows? But if there was technology, you would know right now what's going on.

That's a system failure we can fix.

System Failure #3: The Math That Makes No Sense

Let me tell you about a funding denial that still makes no sense to me.

I was advocating for a woman who was semi-independent. She needed assistance, but she didn't need 24-hour care in her face. Other than needing help with cooking and some medication stuff, she did everything in the house. But she might forget to turn the stove off or forget something while cooking.

So I proposed installing smart technology. Smart knobs. A remote stove that automatically turns off. Or changing out the entire cooktop so burning isn't an option. Or getting a smart cooking device. It's not a ten dollar project, but it's definitely not very expensive when you think about the long run.

Let's say it costs $300 a day to fully serve this person under the current model. By supporting her with technology in a hybrid model, some in-person and majority remote support, the rate could go from $300 a day to $200 a day.

That's saving $100 a day.

Yes, there's an upfront cost of $1,500 to $2,000 to buy the technology that would keep her safe in her home. But you're paying $100 less per day. And you've freed up that physical staff person so they can go support people who need more intensive care.

She was agreeing to it. Everybody was excited.

And then the funding source said no. Because the technology costs too much money.

The technology costs too much money?

I said, but we would be saving $100 a day if we make this purchase. And it might be even more than $100 when she gets more independent and needs even less staff. Eventually she could have a limited amount of staff and more technology. Not 100%, but definitely in a way where she could progress and grow.

Let me do the math for you.

Pay $2,000 for the technology. Save $100 a day. Across a plan year, that's $36,500 in savings.

Don't buy the technology. Spend $36,500 more than you needed to. And continue to create gaps in the staffing crisis because that staff person is stuck there instead of supporting people who actually need intensive physical care.

Pay $2,000, save $36,500.

Or don't pay $2,000, and spend $36,500.

That made no sense. And it still doesn't.

But we're so stuck on parameters, so stuck on "that's expensive for that," without even looking at the logic. We hold up progression. We hold up progress. We hold up independence. We hold up dreams.

Because we're stuck on silly.

"The technology costs too much money." It really didn't. What costs too much money is over-supporting this person when she doesn't need it and under-supporting the people who actually do.

That's a system failure.

System Failure #4: Paperwork Over People

I remember showing an agency how certain technologies have built-in processes where they grab enough data and give you notes automatically. Not to say that's the only note that would be written, but it's a starting point.

The agency was so focused on the fact that they needed staff to write in their own words every 15 minutes. Yes, 15-minute documentation is a thing. I'm not going to get too deep into it, but I'm just going to say it doesn't make sense when the technology can pull data every two minutes if you wanted it to.

But the agency was so focused on getting the every-15-minutes written documentation. And they were using an electronic health record, so it wasn't even handwriting.

What does that mean? That means every 15 minutes, staff have to take their eyes off the person they're supposed to be supporting, stop what they're doing, just so they can go write the note.

And this goes back to what I was talking about earlier. We make up things or we keep things in motion not realizing they put staff in jeopardy. The minute they take their eyes off the situation they're supposed to be paying attention to, and something happens, and there's no technology in place to help explain what occurred, the staff person is in trouble.

They're the ones trying to defend the fact that they were told they have to take time to write the 15-minute increment note when there was clearly a way to do it differently. We could have used voice notes that transfer over to documentation where they wouldn't have to stop doing what they were doing.

But instead, we were so married to a system, a structure that was built when all the technology I just named didn't even exist. We're so married to it that we forget the outcomes we're supposed to be addressing. We just want to see the same old traditional format instead of thinking innovatively about how we could get the same thing with less impact, less trauma, and more positive outcomes.

That's a system failure.

System Failure #5: The Fear of Liability That Creates More Liability

Out of all the questions I get whenever I do presentations around the country, the number one thing I constantly hear is questions around liability. Everyone is afraid of getting in trouble.

I talked about this earlier. The protection from harm framework is really the disability. The disability is not the person supported. The disability is the systems we create. This is what prevents us from being innovative: the fear of getting in trouble, the fear of liability, the fear of what happens when.

But I keep going back to the most serious acute settings. Our hospitals. Those are serious acute settings. An ambulance is a serious acute setting.

Yet their first thing they do is implement the use of technology.

No one is sitting by your bedside in these units. No one. Maybe your family member. But not a nurse or a doctor is sitting by your bedside. Not even a candy striper. Nobody is sitting by your bedside 24/7.

Hospitals are dealing with everything. Life and death. All day long. However, even with that threat, they're still not sitting by your bedside around the clock. They take a risk. They believe in the technology. They rely on the technology. Doctors and nurses rely on the technology.

But for some reason in our field, we tend to think we reduce liability by being fully reliant on an overworked, tired human being.

Humans forget everything. We forget a lot of stuff. We are not robots. We are not superhuman. We are superheroes. But we are not perfect.

Technology is not perfect either. What I'm trying to explain is a union that increases our odds and chances of providing the best support and service and reducing or mitigating risk.

We go all day in a risk posture depending on human beings. I don't know about you, but I'm sure each one of us has met or been that human being that has disappointed a situation. Because we're human.

Technology is an assistant to the human. So when we think about the fear we have about liability and decide not to implement technology because of it, remember that we're asking ourselves to rely on the most unreliable thing on earth.

That's a human being.

A tree is more reliable than a human. Migrating birds are more reliable than a human. And I'm not taking away from humans, but I'm talking about things that just do what they do. A tree is going to do what a tree does until it can't do it anymore. We know that.

But human beings? We have so much going on with us that you never know what you're going to get. I don't even know what you're going to get from me tomorrow. Totally depends on how I feel tomorrow.

That lack of consistency we offer is where the liability actually is.

That's why it should be in our best interest to find ways to incorporate the assistance of technology. To mitigate risk. To reduce liability. To show our insurance companies, hey, look what we got. To show family members, look what we have so we know about things the person can't articulate.

These are the things we should be thinking about.

But it's just amazing how we are more comfortable with not knowing.

That's a system failure.

The Cost of Not Changing

Let me be blunt about what happens if we don't fix these system failures. People suffer. They're placed in wrong settings. They lose independence.

They decline faster than they should. They lose joy. They lose their voice even when they're speaking clearly.

Staff leave. They burn out. They get blamed. They find other careers. The workforce crisis deepens.

Families give up. They stop trusting the system. They stop advocating. They carry burdens alone.

Providers collapse. They can't sustain the staffing model. They can't afford the liability. They close programs. They merge or disappear.

And the future? The future we're all aging into? It looks like 1988 forever.

Unless we choose differently.

Closing: The System Can Change Because We Built It

Here's the truth that gives me hope.

We built these systems. That means we can rebuild them.

The regulations that restrict us? Humans wrote them. Humans can rewrite them.

The cultures that resist change? Humans created them. Humans can transform them.

The funding structures that limit innovation? Humans designed them. Humans can redesign them.

The technology gaps that leave people behind? Humans caused them. Humans can close them.

There is nothing about our current system that is inevitable. Every part of it was a choice. And we can make different choices.

System failures are not permanent unless we decide they are.

The question is: What do we decide?

Do we decide to keep patching 1988?

Or do we decide to build something new?

I've made my decision. I'm building something new.

And I hope you'll join me.

CHAPTER 10: THE POLICY, FUNDING & LEADERSHIP BLUEPRINT FOR TECH EQUITY

Why Innovation Must Be Supported, Understood, and Led With Vision

A Note Before We Begin

I need to be honest with you: this is a policy chapter.

It's going to talk about rate structures, waiver language, regulatory frameworks, and procedure codes. Some of it will feel dry. Some of it will feel rigid. That's the nature of policy.

But here's what I need you to hear before we get into it:

The takeaway from this chapter is not rigidity. It's flexibility.

We need flexibility in rate structures. We need flexibility in rate methodologies. Providers need room to actually implement a person-centered plan of care.

Think about it. If every individual has a fully developed, person-centered plan of care that is truly individualized, you cannot reach that level of individualization while worrying about making sure you have exactly two staff on for eight hours awake and one staff for eight hours overnight. That level of rigidity makes true person-centered care impossible.

When we get too prescriptive, we box ourselves in.

Now, I'm not taking away the need for accountability. We have to show that we are providing services. That's the point of documentation. That's where technology actually helps, because it provides more accurate, more reflective quality data to show that people are healthy and safe. Which, by the way, was the whole intent of those regulations and rigid staffing schedules in the first place.

But we need flexibility to keep this field up and running.

I've seen hospitals offer all kinds of incentives to get nurses to come in. I've seen other industries do creative things to attract and retain workers. But let's be real: this is not the sexy industry where people get discounts for working at a fancy store or free products. We don't have those perks to offer.

What we do have is an opportunity.

An opportunity to make staff fall in love with this work again. An opportunity to advance traditional services into innovative models that actually make sense for delivering person-centered, individualized care. An opportunity to be innovative without being penalized for it.

That's what this chapter is about.

So yes, we're going to talk policy. But the point of the policy is to create space for the innovation that makes this work sustainable.

Let's get into it.

OPENING: The System Was Never Designed for This Moment

The care systems we rely on today, HCBS programs, ICF/IID facilities, nursing homes, assisted living models, and even many community-based frameworks, were not designed for the world we live in now.

They were built in an era when:

- People with disabilities were not expected to live long

- Aging almost always meant institutionalization

- Families were the default caregivers

- Technology barely existed in the care landscape

- The internet was science fiction

- Smart homes were something from The Jetsons

Those systems made sense for a different time.

But the world has changed.

People are living longer.

People are aging with disabilities.

People with disabilities are aging into their 60s, 70s, and 80s.

Medical complexity has become the norm, not the exception.

Family structures have shifted.

DSPs are leaving the workforce at alarming rates.

Technology now shapes every aspect of daily life.

Cultural identity cannot be separated from care.

Autonomy is expected, not requested.

The system has reached a point where it cannot simply be adjusted.

It must be transformed.

This chapter is about the policy, funding, and leadership blueprint needed to support that transformation.

Not because innovation is trendy.

Not because technology is shiny.

But because the math no longer works, and everyone knows it.

SECTION I: Federal Intent Has Always Recognized the Importance of Technology

There is a dangerous misconception floating around this field:

"Technology is new to human services."

"The system isn't set up for this."

"We were never meant to use technology this way."

Let me be very clear:

That is not true.

The federal government recognized the importance of technology in supporting people with disabilities **over fifty years ago.**

Let's look at the timeline.

The Historical Foundation

1973: The Rehabilitation Act

The Rehabilitation Act of 1973 explicitly included "rehabilitation technology, including telecommunications, sensory, and other technological aids and devices" as a type of vocational rehabilitation service that could be provided to eligible individuals (29 U.S.C. § 723).

Read that again.

1973.

Long before smartphones. Long before tablets. Long before the internet was in homes. Long before remote monitoring existed.

The United States government recognized that technology was essential to supporting people with disabilities.

1975: The Education for All Handicapped Children Act

This landmark legislation, signed into law by President Gerald Ford, guaranteed a free appropriate public education for all children with disabilities and mandated that assistive technology be provided as part of that education.

1986: Technology Recognition Expands

Amendments to IDEA began expressly recognizing technology as part of special education services.

1988: The Tech Act

Congress passed the Technology Related Assistance for Individuals with Disabilities Act, dramatically increasing access to and funding for assistive technology for all individuals with disabilities.

1990-1991: IDEA Amendments

The terms "assistive technology device" and "assistive technology service" were formally added to education law, providing clear definitions and mandates.

1997: IEP Requirement

IEP teams became required to consider assistive technology for every student with a disability.

2004: Current IDEA Framework

The mandate was reinforced: IEP teams must consider assistive technology as part of individualized planning.

What This Means

The federal intent has been clear for over fifty years: technology supports equity, access, communication, independence, development, participation, and dignity.

So if we've known this since 1973, why are we still fighting about it in 2025?

Because what we built afterward, the 1988 ICF/IID regulations and many HCBS structures, did not reflect this long-standing legislative direction.

We built models that were:

- Rigid

- Heavily supervision-based

- Resistant to integrated technology

- Focused on physical presence over intelligent design

- Rooted in institutional thinking even when community-based

The gap we are addressing today is not a gap of knowledge.

It is a gap of implementation.

We have known for decades that innovation is essential.

Now we must ensure that funding structures, regulatory frameworks, and leadership practices reflect that truth.

SECTION II: The 1988 Framework That Won't Let Go

Let me tell you something that should concern every leader in this field.

The ICF program itself began in 1971 when Congress enacted legislation establishing federal funding for Intermediate Care Facilities for the Developmentally Disabled as an optional Medicaid benefit. But the current regulatory framework we operate under today, the Conditions of Participation for ICF/IID, was implemented on October 3, 1988.

The last major update to the interpretive guidelines was in 2021.

But that 2021 update? It revised *interpretive guidelines*. It updated the *survey process.*

It did not rebuild the framework.

The 1988 structure remains.

Let that sink in for a moment.

We are operating, in 2025, on a regulatory framework implemented **37 years ago.**

What Was Happening in 1988?

I don't know about you, but I don't have anything from 1988.

Well, I'm lying. I might have my beeper somewhere, but that was probably the early 90s.

In 1988:

- I hadn't even met my husband yet (and we've been together 32 years)

- The internet was not in homes

- Cell phones were the size of bricks and cost $4,000

- "Technology" in disability services meant communication boards and manual wheelchairs

- Remote anything was not even a concept

I can't even imagine still operating my life with the same tools, the same framework, the same assumptions from 1988.

But that's what we're asking people with disabilities to do.

The Core Problem

As I explained in Chapter 1, trying to modernize a 1988 regulatory system is like retrofitting a 1950 Chevy with modern electric vehicle technology. The frame wasn't built for it. We keep patching, adapting, adding exceptions, and wondering why it doesn't work.

SECTION III: Innovation Must Be Supported by Funding Sources Across the Country

Here's where I need to be very careful with my words.

Because in December 2025, talking about Medicaid feels… complicated.

There are threats.

There are cuts coming.

There is uncertainty at every level.

So let me say this clearly:

I am not here to critique Medicaid as a concept.

I am here to say that innovation needs to be supported, encouraged, and expected by funding sources across the country, and that includes Medicaid, Medicare, private insurance, state general funds, and every mechanism we use to pay for care.

The Reality

The issue is not that Medicaid *prohibits* innovation.

In fact, many states already have:

- Procedure codes for technology

- Waiver structures that allow flexibility

- MMIS (Medicaid Management Information Systems) pathways to reimburse enabling technology

- Remote support models approved and operational

The infrastructure exists.

What's missing is:

- Consistent expectation that innovation will be used

- Leadership that prioritizes outcomes over ratios

- Willingness to move away from "this is how we've always done it"

- Understanding that technology is not extra. It's essential

What Innovation Needs

1. Clear Definitions

States need consistent language around:

- Enabling technology

- Remote supports

- Hybrid staffing models

- Tech-enabled independence

- Outcome-based funding

2. Flexible Models

Funding should follow outcomes, not just staffing ratios.

If a person is:

- Safer with technology than without

- More independent with technology than without

- Healthier with technology than without

- Happier with technology than without

Then funding should support that, even if it looks different from the traditional model.

3. Outcome-Driven Thinking

We must shift from:

"Did you have the right number of staff present?"

To:

"Did the person achieve their goals? Are they safe? Are they thriving?"

4. Support for Hybrid Staffing

Technology does not replace people.

It changes how we deploy people.

Funding structures must recognize that a hybrid model, combining technology, remote supports, and in-person care, is not "less service."

It's **smarter service.**

5. Reimbursement Pathways

States need streamlined processes for:

- Technology purchase and installation

- Remote monitoring services

- Data analysis and health tracking

- Training and technical support

6. Training Investment

Innovation requires investment in workforce development.

DSPs, nurses, and managers need training on:

- How to use enabling technology

- How to interpret data

- How to support people with tech tools

- How to troubleshoot and problem-solve

7. Leadership Alignment

State leaders, providers, families, and advocates must be aligned on the vision:

Technology is not the enemy of care. Technology is the future of care.

The Financial Reality

Here's the part people don't want to say out loud:

Innovation is not the expensive option.

It is the sustainable option.

Let me break it down.

Traditional High-Staffing Model:

- Annual cost per person: approximately $237,250

- Staff turnover costs: $3,000-$7,000 per person replaced

- Overtime and emergency coverage: unpredictable and expensive

- Burnout-related quality issues: unmeasurable but real

- When someone is hospitalized, the home cannot bill those days, but the traditional staffing expenses remain the same. That means a reduction in billing for the provider with no reduction in costs.

Hybrid Enabling Technology Model:

- Annual cost per person: approximately $164,250

- Technology installation: $5,000-$15,000 upfront

- Monthly monitoring and infrastructure: $500-$2,000 per month, with most of those costs potentially reimbursable under assistive technology waivers depending on the state

- Physical in-person staffing reduced by 30-50%

- Staff retention improves: fewer turnover costs

Do the math.

A 3-person home under the traditional model costs approximately $711,750 per year.

A 3-person home under the hybrid enabling technology model represents significant savings. For states with modified rate structures, this can mean real budget relief. For providers, the reduction in physical staffing by 30-50% means sustainable operations. Each state is different, but the math works in every scenario I've seen.

And here's what the numbers don't capture:

Technology improves the quality of healthcare data. With better data, we have better opportunities to be proactive. We can identify changes in a person's health before they become emergencies. We can intervene earlier. We can reduce hospitalizations for the unknown.

That's not just cost savings. That's lives protected.

When budgets tighten, innovation is not what should be cut.

Innovation is what ensures the system survives.

SECTION IV: The Resistance From Within: When Systems Fight Their Own Progress

This is the section I need you to sit down for.

Because what I'm about to tell you is the hardest truth in this entire book.

The greatest barrier to innovation is often not federal policy.

It's not the lack of technology.

It's not even the cost.

The greatest barrier to innovation is the internal resistance that surfaces when systems face change.

Let me give you a real example.

The Story

I have sat at tables across the country where:

- A person with a disability expressed a **clear desire** to have enabling technology in their home

- The support team **agreed** it would benefit them

- The funding mechanism to pay for the technology **already existed** in the state's Medicaid system

- The technology model was **lower in cost** than high-level staffing

- The provider had the **skills** to support implementation

- Everyone understood that the model aligned with federal and state directions

Everyone agreed.

The funding was there.

The person wanted it.

The cost was lower.

And yet the answer was still "no."

Why?

The reasons varied, but they all came down to the same core issue:

Fear.

Fear of change.

Fear of the unknown.

Fear of liability.

Fear of doing something differently.

Fear of being the first.

And here's what they said:

"We don't have the money for this."

(False. They had more money allocated for the higher-cost staffing model.)

"They don't need it."

(The person literally said they wanted it.)

"We're not sure it's safe."

(But the person living in a 24/7 staffed home with burnout and turnover *is* safe?)

"We'll think about it."

(Translation: No.)

The Real Problem

The constraints we face are sometimes not because it's not in the regulations.

It's not because it's not in the law.

It's not because there's not a procedure code in MMIS.

It's because we, individually, organizationally, culturally, have placed rigid restrictions on ourselves, and then we impose that same rigid thinking when we sit at someone's circle of support

meeting.

We come to the table with our fears, not their possibilities.

We come with:

- "We've never done it that way"

- "I'm not comfortable with that"

- "That's not how we operate"

- "The state won't like it"

Instead of:

- "What does this person want?"

- "What would make their life better?"

- "How can we make this happen?"

- "Who's already doing this that we can learn from?"

The Shift That's Needed

Leaders must put on their **innovative thinking cap.**

Not their compliance cap.

Not their fear cap.

Not their "this is how we've always done it" cap.

Their innovative thinking cap.

Because if we've known since 1973 that technology is beneficial, and we're still saying "no" in 2025, the problem is not the system.

The problem is us.

SECTION V: How to Write Enabling Technology Into Your State Plan

Alright, state directors and policymakers, this section is for you.

You want to support enabling technology?

Here's how.

The Language Shift: 1988-Era vs. 2025-Era

Let me show you what the shift looks like in concrete terms:

1988-ERA REGULATORY LANGUAGE (Staff-Presence Focused):

> "The residential facility shall maintain staff-to-resident ratios sufficient to ensure the health and safety of residents at all times. Overnight supervision shall be provided by qualified staff physically present in the residence. Staff presence shall be documented every 15 minutes during waking hours."

2025-ERA REGULATORY LANGUAGE (Outcomes-Focused):

> "The residential service shall maintain support systems sufficient to ensure the health, safety, and quality of life of residents through person-centered approaches that may include direct staff support, enabling technology, remote monitoring, and hybrid staffing models as determined by the individual's preferences, assessed needs, and service plan. Safety and well-being outcomes shall be documented through appropriate methods, which may include electronic monitoring, staff observation, and individual self-reporting."

The difference is everything:

- 1988 measures *staff presence*

- 2025 measures *person outcomes*

- 1988 assumes physical presence equals safety

- 2025 recognizes multiple pathways to safety

This is the language shift that must happen at the regulatory level.

Step 1: Update Your Waiver Language

Current language often says:

"Services will be provided by qualified staff in accordance with the Individual Service Plan."

Updated language should say:

"Services will be provided through a combination of qualified staff, enabling technology, remote supports, and hybrid models as determined by the person's preferences, goals, and needs in accordance with the Individual Service Plan."

Add specific service definitions:

Enabling Technology Services: The assessment, installation, monitoring, and maintenance of technology systems that support independence, safety, communication, and community integration, including but not limited to smart home devices, remote monitoring systems, health tracking tools, and communication platforms.

Remote Support Services: Real-time support provided by qualified professionals through audio, video, or digital communication platforms to assist individuals in achieving their goals, maintaining safety, and accessing their communities.

Hybrid Staffing Models: Service delivery approaches that combine in-person direct support, enabling technology, and remote supports to provide person-centered care that maximizes independence while ensuring safety and quality of life.

Step 2: Create a Procedure Code (or Use Existing Ones)

Many states already have codes for:

- Assistive technology assessment

- Durable medical equipment

- Behavioral health technology

- Telehealth services

Expand these or create new codes for:

- Enabling technology assessment and setup

- Monthly remote monitoring

- Technology training for individuals and staff

- Data analysis and reporting

Step 3: Establish Outcome Metrics

Move away from:

- Hours of staff presence

- Number of interventions

- Incident reports

Move toward:

- Person's goal achievement

- Health stability indicators

- Quality of life measures

- Independence levels

- Hospitalization rates

- Community integration participation

- Person and family satisfaction

Step 4: Provide Implementation Support

States should offer:

- Technical assistance for providers

- Training for care managers and service coordinators

- Model programs and pilot initiatives

- Peer learning communities

- Troubleshooting resources

Step 5: Address Liability Concerns

Create clear guidance on:

- Consent processes for technology use

- Data privacy and security standards

- When technology can supplement (not replace) certain supports

- Emergency response protocols

- Quality assurance processes

Clarify that:

- Technology is a tool, not a replacement for human judgment

- Providers using approved technology are not assuming additional liability beyond standard care obligations

- Innovation is expected and supported, not penalized

SECTION VI: The ROI of Enabling Technology (Proof From the Pandemic)

Leaders want proof.

Let me give you something no one can debate.

Before Anyone Had Heard the Word "COVID"

Long before the pandemic, I was catching heat for pushing technology as an option in one jurisdiction. People questioned whether remote supports could really work. They worried about safety. They doubted the model.

But I knew two things:

1. The staffing crisis was only going to get worse.

2. People with disabilities deserved access to their digital community and modern tools of safety.

So I built an emergency backup staffing plan that integrated remote supports, touchless radar sensors, remote health monitoring systems, and overnight health monitoring and presence tech. I tested the technology. I deployed it into homes. I trained staff. I started implementing remote supports across states.

I had no idea COVID was coming.

But when it hit, I was ready.

The COVID Snapshot: 10 Homes, 18 Months, Zero Incidents

When facilities and group homes were converted into supportive living residences almost overnight during the lockdowns, we didn't scramble.

We flipped the switch.

Here's what we implemented across 10 homes (I actually deployed this model in approximately 40 homes, but I'll illustrate with 10):

Why This Example Matters:

During COVID, everyone was home all day. No day programs. No community outings. People supported were in their homes 24/7, which meant residential providers had to staff all day long, not just evenings and overnights.

This is the WORST CASE scenario for staffing costs.

In normal times, people go to day programs during the day, so residential providers typically staff awake hours (4pm-midnight) and overnight. But every time someone stays home sick, has a medical appointment, or day program is closed, the residential provider has to cover that additional staffing. At one point, I remember running 40 medical appointments a week for my residential program. Every one of those appointments meant additional staffing costs that the $450/day rate didn't cover.

So if the remote supports model worked during COVID, when everyone was home all day and staffing costs were at their absolute highest, it works even better under normal circumstances.

The Traditional Model (Before):

- 2-person supportive living residences

- Blended average rate: $550/day per person (this is what the provider bills the funding source)

- Staffing: 2:2 ratio for awake hours (4 p.m. to midnight)

- Staffing: 1:2 ratio for overnight (midnight to 8 a.m.)

- Staff wage: $18/hour average (before any incentives)

Note: During COVID, daytime hours (8am-4pm) when everyone was home were covered through Appendix K companion care, which was an unusual emergency service not typically used. This calculation focuses on the residential staffing we could control and transform.

The Remote Supports Model (During COVID):

- Awake hours (4 p.m. to midnight): Reduced to 1 staff per home

- Overnight (midnight to 8 a.m.): Touchless radar sensors and overnight health monitoring and presence tech monitoring each home

- 1 floating staff covering all 10 homes overnight, supported by remote health monitoring systems

- Remote DSPs monitoring technology alerts

- Tech Navigators checking devices, training staff, and coaching people supported on how to use the technology

The Result:

Over 18 months, this shift unlocked significant reinvestment capacity across those 10 homes.

ROI Calculation Breakdown:

Model	Daily Cost (10 homes)	18-Month Cost (547 days)
Traditional Model	$4,320/day	$2,362,960
Remote Supports Model	$1,584/day	$866,448
Reinvestment Capacity	$2,736/day	**$1,496,592**

Calculation basis: Staff wage $18/hour average. Traditional model per home: 2 staff awake hours (4pm-midnight = 8 hours) + 1 staff overnight (8 hours) = $432/day per home. Remote supports model: 1 staff awake hours per home ($144/home × 10 = $1,440) + 1 floating overnight staff across all 10 homes ($144).

And here's what matters most:

Zero incidents.

During the worst public health crisis in modern history, with lockdowns, fear, staff shortages, and uncertainty everywhere, people were safe. We had real-time data. We knew what was happening in those homes without violating privacy. We looked at risk differently, and we responded differently.

What We Did With the Freed Resources

This is not a story about cutting costs.

This is a story about **flexibility** - the ability to supply supports the way the person needs them, to address gaps in funding, and to innovatively approach health and wellness.

Because we weren't locked into traditional staffing costs, we had options.

We could purchase supplies. We could provide incentives to staff who stayed through the crisis. We increased our capacity to buy more health, wellness, and safety technologies. We had floaters available to assist with shopping and to support quarantine homes when people tested positive.

The resources that would have otherwise been locked in traditional staffing became operational flexibility - the ability to respond, adapt, and invest in what mattered most in the moment.

A Snapshot of Bigger Possibilities

I want to be clear: this is only a snapshot. A short story of big possibilities.

COVID was the most serious situation in my career. If these solutions can work during a global pandemic - with fear, uncertainty, and decimated workforces - then imagine what else we could do as an industry in normal times.

Why This Matters Right Now

With cuts and threats of cuts looming, and inflation eating into every budget, these aren't just nice ideas for the future.

These might be the solutions that allow providers to continue serving people while we fight for better rate structures.

Here's the reality: it takes time to change a policy. It takes time to change a system. Legislative advocacy is important, but it doesn't happen overnight. In the meantime, we still have to support people with dwindling resources.

Remote supports and enabling technology offer flexibility. Not flexibility to do less, but flexibility to do what's actually needed. Flexibility to fill gaps. Flexibility to survive until the system catches up.

That's not abandoning the fight for better funding. That's staying in the fight while making sure people don't fall through the cracks in the meantime.

The Undebatable Proof

If remote supports can work at scale during a global health crisis, with zero incidents, then we can no longer pretend it's "too risky" during normal times.

This wasn't the ideal situation for having to fully execute a plan. Nobody wanted a pandemic. But it proved the point:

Enabling technology works.

Remote supports work.

Hybrid staffing models work.

And when implemented with preparation, training, and the right technology infrastructure, they work **safely.**

When Technology Fails: Why Human Backup Matters

I want to be honest about something: technology doesn't always work perfectly.

During those 18 months, we had moments when the internet went down. We had sensors that needed recalibration. We had power outages that knocked systems offline temporarily.

But here's what happened in those moments: **the human backup protocols kicked in.**

When a sensor lost connection, the remote monitoring team received an alert and immediately dispatched a floating staff member to check on the home. When the internet went down in one area, we had cellular backup systems that took over. When a device malfunctioned, we had trained Tech Navigators who could troubleshoot remotely or dispatch support within minutes.

This is the point.

Enabling technology is not about trusting technology blindly. It's about creating systems where technology and humans work together, where technology handles the routine monitoring, and humans are ready to respond when needed.

The zero incidents we achieved weren't because technology never failed. They were because when technology failed, our human systems were prepared.

Technology enhances safety. Humans guarantee it.

The Authority Arc

Before COVID, I was criticized for pushing technology as an option.

During COVID, providers were struggling to figure out how to keep people safe with decimated workforces.

After COVID, I became the person people called to help them find the solution.

Thank God I never listened to the critics.

What This Means for the Future

The pandemic was a forced pilot program for the entire field. It proved that:

1. **Technology can maintain safety** when physical staffing is reduced

2. **Remote supports can work at scale** across multiple homes

3. **Freed resources can be reinvested** into workforce, quality, and innovation

4. **Preparation matters**: those who had infrastructure in place before the crisis thrived

5. **The old model is not the only model**: we have options

The question is no longer "Can enabling technology work?"

The question is "Why aren't we using it everywhere it makes sense?"

Beyond the Pandemic: The Ongoing Opportunity

The COVID experience demonstrated what's possible. But this isn't just about emergencies.

Every day, providers face:

- Staffing shortages that leave shifts unfilled

- Turnover that drains resources on constant recruitment and training

- Burnout that pushes good DSPs out of the field

- Costs that make quality care unsustainable

Enabling technology addresses all of these. Not by replacing people, but by **releasing them** to do meaningful work while technology handles monitoring, alerts, and overnight presence.

The resources currently locked in 24/7 staffing models could be redirected toward:

- Higher wages for DSPs

- Better training and career development

- More technology that increases independence

- Quality improvements that enhance lives

This isn't about doing less.

It's about doing better.

The ROI That Matters Most

Yes, there are financial benefits to enabling technology. But the real return on investment is measured in:

For People Supported:

- Independence and privacy

- Dignity and choice

- Safety without surveillance

- Quality of life improvements

For Families:

- Peace of mind with real-time information

- Confidence that their loved one is safe

- Connection maintained across distances

For DSPs:

- Meaningful work instead of just occupying shifts

- Protection from burnout

- Tools that make their jobs sustainable

- Career paths that don't dead-end

For Providers:

- Operational flexibility to respond to crises

- Workforce stability in a shortage environment

- Resources to invest in quality and innovation

- Sustainability in an unsustainable system

For the System:

- Proof that alternatives exist

- Models that can scale

- Innovation that serves people

- A path forward that doesn't require infinite staffing

That's not just return on investment.

That's return on humanity.

SECTION VII: Common Objections & Real Responses

Let me address the elephants in every policy room.

OBJECTION 1: "Technology is too expensive."

RESPONSE:

One hospitalization costs more than a year of enabling technology. One year of 24/7 staffing costs 3-4 times more than a hybrid model. The question is not "Can we afford technology?" The question is "Can we afford NOT to use technology?"

OBJECTION 2: "Staff will lose their jobs."

RESPONSE:

We have a workforce crisis. We don't have enough staff. Technology allows us to deploy staff more strategically, pay them better, reduce burnout, and improve retention. Technology doesn't eliminate jobs. It makes jobs more meaningful.

OBJECTION 3: "People don't want to be monitored."

RESPONSE:

Enabling technology is not surveillance. It's support. It's the difference between someone standing in your living room 24/7 versus having a sensor that alerts if you fall. Most people prefer privacy with intelligent backup over constant human presence.

OBJECTION 4: "Our state won't approve it."

RESPONSE:

Many states already have approval pathways. The issue is not state prohibition. It's local fear of trying something new. Connect with states already doing this (ask me for examples).

OBJECTION 5: "We don't have the infrastructure."

RESPONSE:

Neither did anyone else when they started. You build infrastructure by starting small, learning, and scaling. Pilots exist for a reason.

OBJECTION 6: "It's not culturally appropriate."

RESPONSE:

This is why cultural equity must be built into technology from the start. Technology can be more culturally responsive than a rotating workforce that doesn't understand a person's background, language, or values.

OBJECTION 7: "What about privacy concerns?"

RESPONSE:

Current models often have staff in people's bedrooms, bathrooms, and personal spaces 24/7. Technology can provide MORE privacy while maintaining safety. The question is: privacy concerns compared to what?

OBJECTION 8: "We tried remote supports and it didn't work."

RESPONSE:

What didn't work, the technology, the implementation, the training, the person-match, or the organizational resistance? Most "failures" are implementation failures, not technology failures. Learn from what didn't work and try again differently.

SECTION VIII: The Technology First Movement: States Leading the Way

The good news is that this work is already happening across the country.

The "Technology First" movement has been gaining momentum, with states recognizing that technology should be considered first as a natural support to strengthen participation, social inclusion, self-determination, and quality of life for people with disabilities.

What "Technology First" Means

Technology First is a framework where, in person-centered planning, technology including assistive technology, smart home devices, and communication tools is considered first as a way to achieve goals like independence, safety, and community living, rather than as an add-on or afterthought.

States Leading the Movement

Ohio became the first state in 2018 to make Technology First official via executive order, ensuring technology is central to support planning for people with disabilities.

Maryland became a Technology First state in 2022, focusing on meaningful participation, inclusion, and self-determination through technology.

Missouri has a dedicated Technology First Initiative to increase independence and improve quality of life for people with disabilities.

Massachusetts, Oklahoma, Tennessee, and Washington D.C. are leaders in the Advancing States' Enabling Technology Engagement Network (ETEN), expanding access to technology for better outcomes.

New Hampshire, Iowa, and Indiana have made notable legislative efforts to advance Technology First concepts.

The Broader Movement

As of recent counts, over 40 states are engaged in Technology First concepts in some form. The National Association of State Directors of Developmental Disabilities Services (NASDDDS) and ADvancing States have been instrumental in supporting this movement, and the

Enabling Technology Engagement Network (ETEN) continues to bring policymakers, payers, and technology vendors together to align policy and expand technology adoption across aging and disability long-term services and supports.

What This Tells Us

The movement is real. The proof is accumulating. States are demonstrating that when technology is embedded into person-centered planning from the start, people achieve greater independence, providers operate more sustainably, and systems become more resilient.

If your state isn't yet on this list, the question isn't whether Technology First will come to you.

The question is whether you'll help lead it or wait until you have no choice.

SECTION IX: The Leadership Mindset Required for Transformation

Let me close this chapter with the most important part:

Policy doesn't change systems. Leaders do.

You can have the best waiver language in the country.

You can have unlimited funding.

You can have proven technology.

But if leaders don't believe in the vision, nothing changes.

What Transformational Leaders Do

1. They Ask Different Questions

Instead of: "Why should we try this?"

They ask: "Why wouldn't we try this?"

Instead of: "What if it fails?"

They ask: "What if it works?"

Instead of: "We've never done it that way."

They say: "Let's be the first."

2. They Center the Person

Every policy discussion starts with:

"What does the person want?"

"What would improve their life?"

"How do we make that happen?"

3. They Lead With Courage

They're willing to:

- Be the first state/agency/leader to try something

- Make mistakes and learn publicly

- Push back on fear-based objections

- Advocate for change even when it's uncomfortable

4. They Build Bridges

They connect:

- Providers to each other

- Innovators to policymakers

- Families to resources

- Ideas to action

5. They Stay in It

Transformation doesn't happen overnight.

It takes years.

It takes persistence.

It takes showing up even when progress feels slow.

The Question for You

If you're a state director, Medicaid official, provider CEO, or policy leader reading this:

What kind of leader do you want to be?

The one who said "no" when innovation was possible?

Or the one who said "yes" and changed the trajectory of care in your state?

The one who stayed safe and comfortable?

Or the one who built the future?

The choice is yours.

And people are counting on you.

SECTION X: The QIDP Crisis Nobody Is Talking About

There's a gap in our system that nobody is addressing, and it's one of the most critical roles we have.

The QIDP. The Qualified Intellectual Disabilities Professional.

If you work in ICF/IID settings, you know this role by this name. In HCBS settings, the role might be called something different depending on your state, but the functionality is the same. Each state's HCBS waiver application explains how this role is identified, but regardless of what it's called, this is the person responsible for developing and evaluating the individual program plans that determine how people live their lives. They coordinate services. They ensure active treatment requirements are met. They're the bridge between what regulations require and what actually happens in someone's daily life.

It is one of the most important roles in our entire system.

And it is also one of the most under-resourced.

Here's the problem. The regulations tell us we need QIDPs. They tell us what QIDPs are responsible for. But nobody trained QIDPs on the HOW. There's no formal, standardized training that teaches people in this role how to actually develop plans that help someone live their best life. There's no curriculum that bridges the gap between regulatory compliance and person-centered innovation. There's no pipeline preparing the next generation for this work.

We have a critical role operating on a 1988 framework while the rest of the world moves at 2025 speed. The regulations require active treatment, but the people responsible for designing and monitoring that treatment have been given almost no tools to do it well in a digital, technology-enabled environment.

Think about what we're asking QIDPs to do. We're asking them to coordinate complex care. To understand medical needs, behavioral supports, communication systems, family dynamics, cultural considerations, and individual preferences. To develop plans that are both compliant AND person-centered. To evaluate whether those plans are actually working. To adjust and adapt as needs change.

And we're asking them to do it with almost no technology support, no AI tools designed for their context, and training systems that haven't evolved in decades.

This is a workforce development crisis hiding in plain sight.

The Administration for Community Living recently launched the Caregiver AI Competition, recognizing that artificial intelligence can play a role in supporting caregivers and improving outcomes. That federal recognition tells us something important: the need for AI-enabled support in this field is real, and it's being acknowledged at the highest levels.

But here's what I want to make clear. Generic AI will not solve this problem. The Dean Martin Problem applies here too. A QIDP supporting someone with complex needs cannot use a generic chatbot to help develop a person-centered plan. The context is too specific. The regulations are too nuanced. The individual is too unique.

What we need is AI that understands our field. AI trained on person-centered frameworks. AI that can help interpret regulations and translate them into practical, individualized guidance. AI that supports the QIDP role without fragmenting it the way we've fragmented everything else in our system.

This is not a problem I'm just identifying. It's a problem I'm actively working to solve. And I'll say more about that in Chapter 12.

But for now, I want policymakers and state directors to understand this: if we're serious about future-proofing traditional services, we have to invest in the people responsible for making those services work. We have to give QIDPs the training, the tools, and the technology support they need to do this work well.

Otherwise, we're asking people to run a 2025 marathon in 1988 running shoes.

And we already know how that ends.

CLOSING: We Build the Next System Now So We Can Age In It Later

Here's something I think about more than I probably should.

I'm Gen X. I've been in this field for 38 years. And somewhere along the way, I stopped being the young innovator pushing against the old guard and started being the one with gray hairs and decades of experience. Time does that to you.

And now I find myself looking at the system we have and asking a very personal question: Is this where I want to end up?

Because here's the truth that nobody in leadership wants to say out loud. We are all aging. Every single one of us. The state directors making policy decisions today will one day need support. The provider CEOs building programs will one day be on the receiving end of care. The DSPs showing up for shifts will one day need someone to show up for them.

The system we build right now is not just for "them." It's for us. It's for our parents. It's for our children. It's for ourselves.

So when I advocate for enabling technology, I'm not just thinking about the people we serve today. I'm thinking about my own future. I'm thinking about whether I want to age in a system that was designed in 1988, when the internet didn't exist and independence meant something entirely different. Or whether I want to age in a system that honors who I am, respects my choices, uses technology to keep me safe without making me feel watched, and trusts me to live my own life for as long as I possibly can.

That's not a hard choice for me.

And I don't think it's a hard choice for you either.

The work we do in the next five to ten years will determine what care looks like for the next generation. It will determine whether our parents age with dignity or get warehoused in systems that stopped making sense decades ago. It will determine whether our children inherit a field that's sustainable or one that's collapsing under its own weight.

This is not just about policy. Policy is the vehicle, but this is about something much deeper. This is about what kind of world we want to live in. What kind of care we believe people deserve. What kind of legacy we want to leave behind.

I've spent nearly four decades watching this field evolve, and I've seen what happens when people lead with courage versus when they lead with fear. The courageous ones build things that last. The fearful ones protect systems that are already crumbling. And at the end of the day, the people who suffer most from that fear are the ones who have the least power to change it.

So here's what I want to leave you with.

You have more power than you think. Whether you're a state director who can rewrite waiver language, a provider CEO who can pilot a new model, a DSP who can advocate for the people you support, or a family member who refuses to accept "that's just how it is" as an answer. You have the ability to push this field forward. You have the ability to build something better.

And the people who come after you, including future versions of yourself, will thank you for it.

We build the next system now so we can age in it later. That's not a slogan. That's a promise I'm making to myself, and I hope you'll make it too.

Because this work matters. Not just for the people we serve today, but for all of us. For everyone who will ever need care, support, or someone to believe in their ability to live a full life.

That's why I do what I do. That's why I won't stop. And that's why I'm asking you to join me.

CHAPTER 11: BUILDING THE NEXT SYSTEM: A BLUEPRINT FOR TRANSFORMATION

From Philosophy to Practice: How We Actually Do This

OPENING: The Old Systems Did Their Best

Let me start with grace.

The systems we inherited, the ICF regulations from 1988, the HCBS waiver structures, the staffing models, the compliance frameworks, they did the best they could with the tools they had.

They were built by people who cared.

They were designed to solve real problems.

They moved us away from institutions.

They created community living options that didn't exist before.

I honor that work.

But the world has changed.

And systems that don't evolve become barriers to the very people they were designed to serve.

The 1988 framework was not built for:

- Aging in place

- Remote supports

- Enabling technology

- Smart home integration

- Digital health

- Gen X caregivers

- Cultural diversity in care

- Tech-enabled independence

- Staff shortages at this scale

- The aging wave we're experiencing

- New expectations of autonomy

- Humanity-centered services

The system we inherited was built for a different time, a different mindset, and a different understanding of care.

It was built when:

- Institutions were still closing

- Technology meant pagers

- "Independence" was measured by task completion, not choice

- Staff were more available

- People with disabilities weren't expected to live this long

- The internet didn't exist in homes

That system worked for the time it was built in.

It answered the needs of the era.

It was a big step forward from institutionalization.

But the world has evolved.

People have evolved.

Needs have evolved.

Technology has evolved.

Expectations have evolved.

And the system?

It stayed still.

Now it's time to build the next one.

SECTION I: Why We Can't Just "Fix" the Old System

I used this analogy earlier, but it bears repeating:

As I described in Chapter 1, trying to modernize the 1988 system is like trying to retrofit a 1950 Chevy with 2025 Mercedes-Benz EQS technology.

You can try.

You can force new components into old frames.

You can patch and adapt and jury-rig.

And when you're done, it might look impressive.

But:

- It won't function properly

- It will cost more than building something new

- It will frustrate everyone involved

- It will never perform like a system designed for modern needs

We've been doing this for decades.

Patching.

Adapting.

Adding interpretive guidelines.

Creating exceptions and workarounds.

Trying to fit 2025 lives into 1988 structures.

It's not working.

The workforce is collapsing.

The costs are unsustainable.

The outcomes are inconsistent.

The people we serve are demanding more.

The families are exhausted.

The providers are burning out.

We don't need another patch.

We need a new blueprint.

SECTION II: The Five Principles of the Next System

The next system must be built on a fundamentally different foundation.

Not compliance-first. Not surveillance-first. Not cost-first.

Humanity-first.

Let me walk you through the five principles that I believe must guide everything we build going forward.

PRINCIPLE 1: Person-Led, Not System-Led

I have sat in too many ISP meetings where the conversation starts with "Here's what we offer" instead of "What do you want?" The system determines what's available, and then the person is expected to fit themselves into those boxes. That's backwards.

In the next system, the person determines what they want, and then we figure out how to make it happen. Services get designed around the individual's goals, preferences, culture, and dreams. Not around program requirements.

What does this actually look like? It looks like ISP meetings that start with genuine questions about what the person envisions for their life. It looks like technology options being presented as possibilities, not prescribed as the only answer. It looks like cultural preferences actually shaping how services get delivered. It looks like the person being able to say "no" without being penalized or labeled as non-compliant.

The shift is simple to say and harder to do: we move from "What does the system allow?" to "What does the person need, and how do we make it happen?"

PRINCIPLE 2: Technology-Enabled, Not Technology-Replaced

This is where I need to be really clear, because this is where the fear lives.

The old way of thinking treats technology as a replacement for human care. It's seen as a cost-cutting measure that reduces staff and cheapens services. And I understand why people are afraid of that, because in some cases, that's exactly how technology has been misused.

But that's not what enabling technology is about.

Technology should be seen as an enhancement to human care. It's a tool that extends what's possible, fills gaps, and frees staff to do meaningful work instead of just occupying shifts. Technology handles the monitoring so that staff can handle the connection. Sensors detect problems, but humans solve them. Data informs decisions, but relationships drive them.

When done right, the person actually has more support, not less. It just looks different than a body standing in the room.

The shift is from "technology or people" to "technology and people, working together."

PRINCIPLE 3: Culturally Rooted, Not Culturally Blind

I've already talked about this throughout the book, but it bears repeating here because it has to be baked into the foundation of whatever we build next.

The old way designs services for a generic "person" who doesn't actually exist. Culture, language, identity, and history are afterthoughts. Or they're not thought of at all.

The next system has to be different. Services need to be designed with culture at the center. Technology needs to adapt to the person, not the other way around. Staff need training in cultural humility. Identity needs to be honored, not erased.

What does this look like practically? It looks like technology interfaces available in multiple languages. It looks like Deaf individuals having visual alerts, not just audio. It looks like Black elders' historical distrust of surveillance being respected and addressed, not dismissed. It looks like immigrant families' values shaping how services get delivered. It looks like neurodivergent individuals having sensory-appropriate options. It looks like cultural foods, traditions, and practices being supported rather than ignored because they don't fit the meal plan template.

The shift is from "one size fits all" to "one size fits one."

PRINCIPLE 4: Autonomy-Centered, Not Risk-Obsessed

I've watched this field become paralyzed by fear. Every decision gets filtered through "What could go wrong?" Freedom is treated as a liability. Safety and autonomy get positioned as opposites, as if you can only have one or the other.

That's a false choice.

In the next system, decisions need to be filtered through a different question: "What could go right?" Freedom needs to be treated as a human right. Safety and autonomy need to be understood as partners, not enemies.

What does this look like? It looks like risk assessments that include "What's the risk of NOT trying this?" It looks like people being supported to take calculated risks that align with their goals. It looks like "dignity of risk" being actually practiced instead of just quoted in trainings. It looks like failure being treated as learning rather than liability. It looks like decisions being made with the person, not for them.

The shift is from "How do we keep them safe from life?" to "How do we keep them safe to live?"

PRINCIPLE 5: Predictive and Preventative, Not Reactive

The old system waits for crisis. Something goes wrong, then we respond. Hospitalizations happen, then we adjust. Decline occurs, then we notice.

That's not good enough anymore.

The next system needs to anticipate and prevent. Technology gives us the ability to detect patterns early. Intervention can happen before crisis. Health can be stabilized, not just treated after it falls apart.

What does this look like? It looks like sleep patterns being monitored so that disruption triggers check-ins before exhaustion causes bigger problems. It looks like vital sign trends being tracked so that doctors get consulted before hospitalization is needed. It looks like behavioral patterns being analyzed so that support gets adjusted before escalation. It looks like fall risk being detected so that the environment gets modified before injury. It looks like decline being caught early so that life gets extended with quality, not just quantity.

The shift is from "What happened?" to "What's about to happen, and how do we prevent it?"

SECTION III: The Five Phases of System Transformation

Principles are important, but leaders need a roadmap. So let me walk you through the five phases of transforming from the old system to the new one. These aren't rigid timelines because every organization is different, but they give you a sense of the journey.

PHASE 1: ASSESS

Before you can build something new, you have to take an honest look at where you are right now. And I mean honest. Not the version you put in grant applications. The real picture.

This is where you ask the hard questions. What technology do we currently use, and is it actually working? How are we deploying staff, and what does that really cost us? What are our outcomes when it comes to quality of life, health, and satisfaction? Where are our gaps? And most importantly, what do the people we support actually want?

The actions in this phase are about gathering information. Conduct a technology inventory. Survey the people receiving services, and actually listen to what they tell you. Survey your staff, because they see things leadership often misses. Analyze your cost data. Identify who might be good candidates for a pilot. And assess whether your organizational culture is ready for change or whether you're going to face resistance.

The outcome of this phase is clarity. A clear picture of your current state and your readiness for transformation.

PHASE 2: VISION

Once you know where you are, you need to define where you're going. What does the future look like for your organization specifically? Not some generic vision statement that could apply to anyone, but a real picture of what care will look like in five years if you do this right.

This is where you ask questions like: What role will technology play? How will we deploy staff differently? What outcomes will we measure? How will we involve people we support in the design process? What cultural values will guide us?

The actions in this phase are about building alignment. Convene a transformation team that includes people with disabilities, families, DSPs, and leadership. Develop a vision statement that actually means something. Define what success looks like in measurable terms. Create a communication plan so everyone knows what's happening and why. Identify champions at every level of the organization. And address fears and resistance openly, because if you don't, they'll sabotage you later.

The outcome of this phase is a shared vision that the entire organization understands and believes in.

PHASE 3: IMPLEMENT

Now here's where I'm going to push back on the traditional approach, because I have a different philosophy about pilots.

The conventional wisdom says start small. Pick three to five homes. Test carefully. Move slow. And I understand the logic behind that. But here's what I've learned after decades in this field: our system moves so slow that if we take the traditional pilot approach, we'll still be piloting in ten years. We keep going back. We keep waiting. We keep studying. Meanwhile, the future is passing us by.

Let me tell you a story. It was 2011. I remember it specifically because it was the same year we had that earthquake in the DMV area. I had just finished learning from a pioneer in Indiana who was doing things differently, and I was so excited to bring those ideas back. I went to the director and said, have you considered how we might add these innovative solutions to the mix? We were literally sitting in meetings talking about staffing struggles and quality outcomes, and I thought this was the perfect time to explore something new.

She wasn't against it. But it wasn't pushed. And so every single year when we met to review the assistive technology waiver, I brought it up. For years I walked around with a CD in my bag showing people learning how to use technology. I wanted to demonstrate that this wasn't just me going rogue. It was a real approach that could fill gaps in care.

And you know what was happening during that same time? Everyone was worried about Facebook safety. Meanwhile, everybody and their mother and grandmother was on Facebook. But we were hand-wringing about whether someone with a disability should have a Facebook account so they could stop having those awful pen pal goals that should have died out years ago. That was the level of resistance we were dealing with.

So when I talk about Phase 3, I'm not talking about grabbing three or five people and testing for a few months. That approach is played and old. Nobody serious does transformation that way anymore.

My approach is to implement foundational baseline technology across the board.

Unless someone completely rejects knowing more about their own health, which usually doesn't happen. Most people want to know what's going on with their body. Most parents definitely want to know what's happening with their baby. So you implement baseline foundational things around health monitoring. Fall detection. Vital signs. Sleep patterns. You implement these across the board.

Why? Because you need to build confidence in the technology. You need to show its value. You need to demonstrate how technology helps the human. The human needs to be able to say, "I never could have learned that just with my human eyes."

That's what starts to build confidence in the next way we approach IDD services.

It cannot be just start with one smartwatch and give it to somebody. That doesn't work. The same way when we closed the institutions, we didn't just tell one person to go out and see how it goes and come back to let us know whether the institution is better. No. We had to move. If we would have done one by one out of the institutions, we would still be in them because our system is so traditional and so slow to move.

This requires courage. It requires us to stick our chest out, put our shoulders back, and say we're doing it.

Think about what we already have in place that nobody questions. We have scales. We have blood pressure cuffs. Those are health monitoring tools. And now we have scales and blood pressure monitors that automatically send data to an app and record all the information. No one questions that. So there's nothing more to question about another piece of technology that can alert if someone falls. We have to know about falls anyway. That's why we have these staffing ratios in the first place.

We're not saying something foreign or so far removed from what exists. What we're doing is translating a very traditional service to the next normal. The next innovative normal. The next way we approach IDD services.

And it's coming whether we like it or not.

The question I always ask during my presentations is this: The future is here. It's coming and it's already here. My question is, have we prepared the future for us?

I don't want to see us keep having to go back to recreate. It's chaos. I've been doing this long enough to tell you that it is a lot of chaos to have one part of your organization operating one way and another part operating differently. You implement foundational things that help with something you're already regulated and obligated to do: monitor health and wellness. Then you start teaching and getting buy-in on how valuable that is for helping people live their best life.

That is the pilot I'm talking about. You implement the foundational baseline. Then you build up the person-centered technology that goes along with individuals one by one. But the foundation is set in stone. It's already proving quality outcomes and providing quality data and showing families, regulators, overseers, and service coordinators that somebody is healthy and safe.

We're not guessing anymore. We're not taking people randomly to the doctor with no information saying "something's wrong." Imagine if you can take actual data about what's happening to this person. Even if they can't communicate verbally, their body is communicating. You can say to the clinician, "Can you look at this data and based on what you see, run your own tests?"

That's what we want to get out of this. We do not want to move slow.

So when I say implement, I'm not talking about grabbing three people and hoping for the best. I'm a cold turkey person. Let's go. Either we're going to do it or we're not. And I'm saying we're going to do it because the future is coming. It's already here.

The outcome of this phase is not proof of concept. You already know the concept works. The outcome is organizational transformation with data to back it up.

PHASE 4: GROW AND PERSONALIZE

Once you've built your foundational infrastructure and you're seeing the value of baseline health monitoring across your organization, this is where you start evaluating what you're learning and looking for more ways to match individuals with technology that fits their specific needs and goals.

The foundation is set. Now you grow from it.

This phase is about two things happening at the same time. First, you're looking at the data coming from your foundational technology and asking what it's teaching you. What patterns are you seeing? What's working? What needs adjustment? You're learning from what you implemented and refining as you go.

Second, and this is the person-centered part, you start building up individualized technology solutions one person at a time. The baseline is the same for everyone. But now you're asking: what does this specific person need beyond the foundation? Maybe someone wants more independence in their morning routine. Maybe someone wants better communication tools. Maybe someone's health data is showing something that needs a specialized response. This is where you get into the one-by-one work of matching technology to individual goals.

And this is also where you really need to figure out how your remote team and your hybrid team work together. Because now you have staff who are physically present and staff who are monitoring from afar, and they need to function as one coordinated system. How does the remote team communicate with the in-person team? What are the handoff protocols? Who responds to what kind of alert? How do you make sure nothing falls through the cracks? This is operational work that has to be figured out and documented.

The IT infrastructure matters here too. You need systems that can handle the data flow. You need reliable connectivity. You need backup protocols for when technology fails. Your IT team should be actively involved in troubleshooting and strengthening what you've built.

The questions in this phase are about learning and personalizing. What is the data telling you about health patterns across your organization? Which individuals are ready for more technology that supports their specific goals? How are your remote and in-person teams coordinating? Where are the communication gaps? What infrastructure needs strengthening?

The actions are about refinement and expansion. Develop clear protocols for how remote and in-person staff work together. Train staff on interpreting and responding to technology data. Create individual technology plans that build on the foundation. Strengthen your IT infrastructure based on what you've learned. Build internal expertise so you're not dependent on outside consultants forever. And keep measuring, because you're never really done.

The outcome of this phase is a mature system where foundational technology is running smoothly, individualized technology is being added based on person-centered goals, and your remote and hybrid teams are working together seamlessly.

PHASE 5: SUSTAIN

The final phase isn't really final because it never ends. This is where you embed the new approach into your organizational DNA so that it becomes just how you do things, not a special project.

The questions in this phase are about longevity. How do you maintain what you've built? How do you continue improving? How do you onboard new staff into this culture? How do you stay current with technology changes? How do you keep the person at the center as you grow? How do you share what you've learned with others in the field?

The actions are about institutionalizing change. Integrate technology into all training for new hires. Build continuous improvement processes. Share success stories internally and externally. Mentor other organizations that are starting their journey. Advocate for policy changes based on your experience. Stay connected to innovation in the field. And never stop asking the most important question: "What do the people we support want?"

The outcome of this phase is a transformed organization that continues evolving.

SECTION IV: Who Needs to Be at the Table

Transformation fails when the wrong people are making decisions. Or when the right people are left out of the room.

Let me tell you who needs to be involved, and I'm going to be specific about why each group matters.

People with disabilities have to be at the table. Not as tokens. Not as guests who get invited to one meeting and then never heard from again. As leaders. They are the experts on their own lives. They must be at every table, in every meeting, shaping every decision. If you're building a system for people with disabilities without people with disabilities in the room, you're already doing it wrong.

Families need to be there too. They bring perspective, history, and accountability. They know things that staff don't know. They remember things that get lost in documentation. And here's the truth: families can be your biggest advocates or your biggest obstacles. If you include them early and genuinely, they'll fight alongside you. If you exclude them or treat them as afterthoughts, they'll fight against you.

Direct Support Professionals are essential. They know what actually happens on the ground. They see the gaps that leadership never sees. They have ideas that never make it up the chain. They need to be heard and valued, not just informed of decisions that have already been made.

Clinicians and nurses bring the health perspective. They understand the medical needs and can help design systems that actually improve health outcomes rather than just documenting them.

Your IT team needs to be at the table as reinforcers of the infrastructure. This is not optional. They're the ones who will keep the technology running. They're the ones who will troubleshoot when things break. They're the ones who understand connectivity, data security, and system integration. If you don't include IT from the beginning, you'll build something they can't support, and then you'll wonder why it keeps falling apart. IT isn't just a service department you call when something breaks. They're partners in building and maintaining the foundation.

Technology partners matter because they know what's possible. They can help you avoid expensive mistakes. But choose carefully. You want partners who understand your mission, not just vendors who understand their sales goals.

Finance and operations people need to be at the table because they can help you build sustainable models. They need to see the ROI and understand the investment timeline. If you don't bring them along, they'll kill your transformation with budget objections.

Leadership sets the tone and allocates resources. They must be visibly committed, not just verbally supportive. There's a difference between a CEO who says "I support this" and a CEO who shows up to pilot site visits and asks questions.

Board members provide governance and accountability. They need to understand and support the transformation, or they'll get nervous when things get hard and pull the plug.

And state partners control the funding, policy, and oversight. Bring them along as allies early. If you wait until you need approval to engage them, you've waited too long.

SECTION V: Common Pitfalls and How to Avoid Them

I've seen transformations fail. I've watched organizations start strong and then crash. I've seen millions of dollars wasted and years of effort abandoned. So let me tell you what goes wrong and how to prevent it.

The first pitfall is starting with technology instead of people. This happens all the time. An organization gets excited about a new device or platform, buys a bunch of equipment, and then tries to figure out who to use it with. That's backwards. Technology is a tool, not a solution. If you start by buying devices before understanding what people need, you'll waste money and lose trust. Start with listening instead. What do people want? What are their goals? What would improve their lives? Then find the technology that supports those answers.

The second pitfall is not involving staff early enough. If DSPs feel like technology is being done to them instead of with them, they will resist. Sometimes they'll resist passively by just not using the technology correctly. Sometimes they'll resist actively by sabotaging it. I've seen it happen. The way to avoid this is to involve DSPs from day one. Ask for their input. Address their fears directly. Show them how technology makes their jobs better, not obsolete. Make them champions of the change rather than victims of it.

The third pitfall is underestimating the culture change required. This isn't just about installing sensors. It's about changing how people think about care, independence, risk, and their own roles. That kind of change doesn't happen because you send an email or hold a training. It requires serious investment in change management. Communicate constantly. Address resistance directly rather than hoping it goes away. Celebrate small wins to build momentum. And be patient, because culture change takes years, not months.

The fourth pitfall is trying to do everything at once. Organizations that try to transform everything simultaneously usually end up transforming nothing. The energy gets dispersed, the focus gets lost, and nothing gets done well. Start small instead. Pick pilots you're confident can succeed. Build momentum before scaling. Learn as you go. There's no shame in starting with two homes instead of twenty.

The fifth pitfall is declaring victory too early. One successful pilot is not transformation. I've seen organizations celebrate a pilot, put out a press release, and then watch the whole thing fall apart when they try to scale. Sustainability requires ongoing attention. Build systems for continuous improvement. Keep measuring even after the pilot phase is over. Stay humble. The work is never "done."

The sixth pitfall is ignoring the policy environment. If your state doesn't support what you're doing, you're going to hit walls. You might implement something brilliant, and then get cited for it in a survey. The way to avoid this is to engage state partners early. Advocate for policy changes. Document your outcomes meticulously so you can build the case. Be a leader in the policy conversation rather than waiting for permission.

SECTION VI: Measuring Success

You can't improve what you don't measure. But you also have to measure the right things.

For too long, this field has measured compliance instead of outcomes. We've measured whether staff were present instead of whether people were thriving. We've counted hours instead of counting what actually matters.

So let me tell you what you should be tracking.

On the person-centered side, you want to look at quality of life scores, goal achievement rates, and satisfaction. How independent are people becoming? How much are they participating in their communities? Do they feel like they have real choice and control over their lives?

On the health side, track hospitalization rates and ER visits. Look at medication management accuracy. Count early detection events, the times when technology or monitoring caught something before it became a crisis. Watch for health stability indicators that tell you whether people are doing better over time.

On the workforce side, measure staff retention rates and turnover costs. Look at staff satisfaction and burnout indicators. Track training completion, not just whether people attended but whether they're actually using what they learned.

On the financial side, look at cost per person and technology ROI. Calculate avoided costs from prevented hospitalizations, prevented crises, and reduced turnover. Watch your margin improvements and sustainability indicators.

And at the system level, track your implementation timeline. Are you hitting your milestones? What's your pilot success rate? How is scaling progressing? Have you achieved any policy changes based on your work? Are you influencing the broader field?

The point isn't to drown in data. The point is to know whether what you're doing is actually working, and to have the evidence to prove it when someone asks.

SECTION VII: The Courage Required

Let me close this section with the truth nobody wants to say.

Building the next system requires courage. Real courage. The kind that costs you something.

It requires the courage to try something new when the old way is comfortable and familiar. It requires the courage to invest in technology when budgets are tight and everyone is asking where the money is going. It requires the courage to challenge regulations that don't make sense, even when you know it might create friction with the people who enforce them. It requires the courage to listen to people with disabilities when the system is telling you to do something different. It requires the courage to push back on fear-based objections from people who have more power than you. It requires the courage to be the first in your state or region, knowing that being first means being watched and scrutinized. It requires the courage to fail publicly and learn from it rather than hiding your mistakes. And it requires the courage to keep going when progress feels painfully slow.

Transformation is not for people who need everything to feel safe before they move. It's for leaders who believe that people deserve more than survival. It's for people who understand that the old system is failing and who refuse to keep pretending otherwise. It's for those who see technology as a tool for freedom rather than control. It's for people who are willing to take risks for the right reasons and who can hold a long-term vision while taking short-term action.

If that's you, then you're ready.

And I'm here to help.

CLOSING: We Build the Next System Now So We Can Age In It Later

I've said this before, but it bears repeating here because it's the thread that ties everything together.

The system we build now is the system we will live in when we age.

I think about this constantly. I'm Gen X. I've been doing this work for nearly four decades. And I'm not that far from the day when I might need support myself, whether for aging, disability, or both.

When that day comes, I don't want to be placed in a system that was designed in 1988. I don't want to be watched instead of supported. I don't want to be controlled instead of trusted. I don't want to be warehoused in a model that stopped making sense before most of my staff were born.

I want to age in a system that honors my humanity. That respects my autonomy. That uses technology to keep me safe without making me feel surveilled. That understands my culture and my identity. That sees me as a whole person with a lifetime of experiences, not just a set of needs to be managed.

And if I want that for myself, I better make sure I'm building it for everyone else.

The next system has to be designed with autonomy at its center. With identity and culture woven throughout. With technology as a tool for freedom. With community as the goal. With workforce sustainability so that the people providing care aren't burning out and leaving. With dignity as the floor, not the ceiling. With equity so that everyone has access, not just those who can afford it. With humanity as the foundation for every decision.

Because the system we build won't just determine other people's lives today. It will determine our own lives as we age. It will determine what happens to our parents. It will determine what our children inherit.

This is not just policy. This is not just program design. This is not just innovation for innovation's sake.

This is a movement. And you are part of it, whether you realized it before picking up this book or not.

STORY: "I Finally Got My Legs"

I need to tell you about an agency that didn't wait for permission.

Because the next system isn't just a vision I'm describing. It's already being built. Right now. By people who decided that innovation wasn't optional. It was essential.

There's an organization in Spartanburg, South Carolina called Charles Lea. They're a large provider, but what I love most is their innovation unit, specifically the work being done under a man named Omar Chirinos. Every time I visit them, it feels like a family reunion. Every time I spend time with them, it feels like coming home to kindred spirits.

I call everybody cousin. And the cousins at Charles Lea? They're my people.

Because they don't see limitations. They don't ask "Why?" They ask "Why not?" They don't say "Let's study it." They say "Let's try it. Let's see what it can do. Let's get it done."

My spirit gets attracted immediately to that kind of energy.

And they are living proof that the future we're building is not just possible. It's already here.

There's a man they support named Anthony.

Anthony has significant physical needs. The kind of needs that an average system would look at and say, "He needs total care. He needs staff 100% of the time. He needs around-the-clock supervision."

And Anthony has one of those mamas.

You know the kind I'm talking about. The kind of mama who can control you from across the church while she's singing in the choir and you're cutting up in the back pew. All she has to do is give you that look and you get yourself together. That kind of mama.

She don't play no games.

And when her son, her baby, said he wanted to move from 100% direct assistance to being supported remotely, to only receiving help when he called or when he needed it, she was not having it.

"I don't know what y'all talking about. Not my baby. Y'all better be on that shift."

I know a lot of mamas like that. Whether their child has a disability or not. That protective love. That fierce guardianship. That refusal to let anything happen to her child on her watch.

But over time, the team at Charles Lea helped show her what was possible. They didn't dismiss her fears. They addressed them. They didn't push past her concerns. They walked through them with her.

And Anthony, for his part, found the words to say: "Mama, let me give it a try."

What mama doesn't want to be able to say yes to her child?

She agreed. Reluctantly. With conditions. And she was right on their neck every step of the way.

"Let something happen to my baby, y'all gonna catch it. Y'all gonna catch these hands."

But nothing happened. Except progress.

Over time, Anthony went from needing 100% support to only needing drop-in support. This man, who by every regulatory standard would be classified as requiring total care, was living independently with technology-enabled support.

And he was thriving.

The last time I visited Charles Lea, Anthony came in to give us an update.

But something was different.

Before, he had a custom manual wheelchair. Beautiful, but it still required staff to push him around. He couldn't move independently. He had to wait for someone else to take him where he wanted to go.

This time?

This time he rolled in controlling a power wheelchair with his head.

I looked at him and said, "Oh my God, Anthony! Where'd you get this Cadillac from? You got the Range Rover of wheelchairs!"

He just smiled.

He told us about the learning curve. How at first he almost ran over a whole bunch of people at the day program. How if it were a car on the street, he might've gotten some citations. But eventually, he got the hang of it.

And during my visit, I watched him parallel park that wheelchair better than most people parallel park their cars.

With his head movements.

I've been watching Anthony's journey for a while now. And every time he adds something new, every time technology opens another door for him, it feels personal. It feels like his wins are my wins.

Because when you've invested your heart in this work, you carry people's stories with you.

Then came the moment.

Anthony was telling us about this new chair. About what it meant to him. About the people who believed in him when the world said he couldn't.

And then he said something I will never forget.

He said:

"With this wheelchair, I finally got my legs."

I lost it.

I am crying right now telling you this story.

This man, who was born into a body that the world said would confine him, who was placed in a system that said he would always need total care, who was surrounded by regulations that could have limited his possibilities, this man finally got his legs.

Because technology entered the picture.

Because innovative minds entered the picture.

Because an agency like Charles Lea and a leader like Omar Chirinos didn't wait for permission.

Because a mama who loved her baby fierce enough to be afraid also loved him fierce enough to let him try.

Because Anthony himself never stopped believing that more was possible.

If Anthony can do it, everybody can do it.

That's not just a slogan. That's truth.

That's the next system.

That's what we're building.

There is no greater moment than seeing someone live out their best life when everything around them told them it wasn't possible.

That's why I can't stop.

That's why I do what I do.

That's why I advocate.

That's why I push.

That's why I use my abilities to break down barriers so that everybody's abilities can enter the space.

If Anthony can do it, everybody can do it.

Remember that.

Your Monday Morning: Where to Start

You've read the vision. You've seen the frameworks. Now let me give you something practical, because I know how overwhelming transformation can feel when you're staring at a full inbox on Monday morning.

Here's the thing: you don't have to do everything at once. But you do have to start somewhere. So let me tell you where to start depending on your role.

If you're a Provider CEO or Agency Leader, your first move is to figure out how you can get some baseline foundational training for your organization. How do you start setting up your remote team? How do you start preparing for being able to provide services from afar? This is a shift in thinking, going from that caregiver model where everyone is physically present to a model where you can be there without being there. How do you run an ISP goal from afar? How do you respond to technology? How do you respond to the data that's coming from technology? How do you coordinate with circles of support, whether the nurse, the home manager, the QIDP? You need to start working on that because this is your foundational structure. This is what's necessary for your future organization to stand on, and you will grow from it. It might not look the same five years from now, but it'll be nothing if you don't start.

If you're a State Director or Policymaker, I want you to pull your current waiver language on staffing requirements and really examine it. There's nothing wrong with physical presence requirements. I appreciate that. I prefer a more hybrid model, but I understand the intent behind physical presence. What I want you to ask is: does your language allow for hybrid models, or does it require physical presence in ways that are limiting? Is physical presence mandatory in all circumstances, or is there flexibility? How does an agency have autonomy to implement staffing based on the needs of that particular day, as long as they stay within the needs of the person and what's documented in the ISP? These are the questions that matter.

And here's another thing for state directors: how are you improving workforce development? How are you helping DSPs prepare for the future? How are you preparing for the newer generation of DSPs who might never have had experience being a traditional caregiver or working side by side in person, but who have extensive technology experience? What kind of training are you going to offer them so they have real skills, not just theory or ideologies, but actual functional skills they can use on day one?

If you're a DSP or Direct Care Staff, start by having a real conversation with one person you support about what independence means to them. Not what independence means to the system. What it means to them personally. Listen to what they say. Then ask yourself: is there anything we're doing right now that gets in the way of that? And is there any technology that might help? You don't have to have the answers. Just start noticing. And start thinking about what your role looks like in a world where technology handles some of the monitoring so you can focus on the relationship.

If you're a Family Member, ask your loved one's provider a direct question: "Are you using any enabling technology, and if not, why not?" Their answer will tell you a lot about where they are on this journey. If they're not using technology, ask what it would take to explore it. If they seem resistant, ask what they're afraid of. Sometimes just asking the question plants a seed.

If you're a Person Receiving Services, tell your team what you want. I know that sounds simple, but it's actually the most powerful thing you can do. Tell them what independence looks like for you. Tell them what you wish you could do that you can't do right now. Tell them what would make your life better. Your voice matters more than anyone else's in this conversation, and sometimes the system forgets that until you remind them.

Transformation doesn't start with a strategic plan or a budget approval. It starts with one person deciding that things could be different and taking one step in that direction.

What will your step be?

CHAPTER 12: THE CALL TO ACTION: I Got You

OPENING: The Moment That Changed Everything

There comes a moment in every person's life when their calling introduces itself. Not with trumpets or fanfare, but with a quiet whisper that says, "This is why you're here."

For some people, that moment comes in a boardroom.

For others, it comes in a classroom.

For me, it came in a YMCA pool in Jamaica, Queens, when I was fourteen years old.

I didn't know it then, but that moment would shape the next thirty-eight years of my life. It would become the foundation of every innovation I've created, every person I've supported, every system I've challenged, and every word in this book.

Let me take you there.

SECTION I: When Everyone Else Said No

It was a regular day at the YMCA on Parsons Boulevard. I was a junior lifeguard, young, confident, maybe a little fearless in the way that only fourteen-year-olds can be. The kind of confidence that comes from not yet knowing all the ways things can go wrong.

That day, an organization called United Cerebral Palsy of Queens, UCP, came to the YMCA with a request. They wanted to bring some adults from a nearby ICF, a group home, to experience the water. These were wheelchair users with cerebral palsy, people with spastic conditions that limited their range of motion, people whose bodies moved in ways that most folks weren't used to seeing.

They wanted to bring them to the pool.

But there was a problem.

Actually, there were several problems.

The YMCA didn't have an accessible pool. This was an old building. No ramps, no lifts, no accommodations. The elevators didn't even fit some of the wheelchairs, so we had to bring people through the side entrance.

And when UCP asked if we could help get these folks into the water, every single lifeguard on duty that day said no.

Not because they were mean.

Not because they didn't care.

But because they were afraid.

Afraid of hurting someone.

Afraid of the unknown.

Afraid of doing something they had never done before.

If you've never worked with someone who has significant physical disabilities, someone with equipment and medical needs you don't understand, that fear is real. Nobody wants to cause harm. Nobody wants to be the reason something goes wrong.

So they said no.

But I didn't.

SECTION II: I'll Do It

"I'll do it," I said.

The other lifeguards looked at me like I was out of my mind.

"You're just a junior lifeguard," they said.

"Yeah," I said. "But you guys are here. I'll do it."

I didn't know what I was doing. I had no special training. I had never worked with anyone with cerebral palsy. I had no manual, no certification, no step-by-step guide.

But I had something else.

I had my grandmother's voice in my head:

"If you have a talent, Precious, you use it to help someone else. And when you do that, God will bless you beyond your imagination."

And I had common sense:

I'm in the pool. They're buoyant. I'm buoyant. We're in the shallow end. What could possibly happen?

So I said yes.

SECTION III: The First Time

They lowered the first person into the water.

We had to do it by hand. There was no accessible ramp, no mechanical lift. Just human hands and human care.

I remember standing in that shallow end, waist-deep in water, looking at her as the other lifeguards carefully lowered her toward me.

She was looking at me.

I was looking at her.

We were both thinking the same thing:

I guess we're going to figure this out together.

Her body was tight. Constricted. The muscle spasms that came with her condition made her movements stiff and unpredictable. I could see the tension in her face. Not from pain, but from uncertainty.

She didn't know me.

I didn't know her.

But we were about to trust each other in a way that required more than words.

So I started talking.

Softly. Gently. The way my grandmother used to hum when she was thinking through something important.

"I got you," I whispered.

"Just relax. Don't worry. I got you."

"Pretend like you're laying in your bed, looking up at the stars. Nothing is going to happen to you."

"I got you."

I kept saying it. Over and over.

I got you. I got you. I got you.

And as I held her, my arm supporting her back, the water holding her weight, I felt her body begin to change.

The tension started to release.

Her muscles began to soften.

Her breathing slowed.

She put her head back.

And then I saw it.

A smile.

Not a big, showy smile. Not laughter or words.

Just a quiet, peaceful, joyful curve at the corner of her mouth.

She didn't have verbal words to speak.

But I heard everything.

I heard every ounce of joy in her face. I heard her relief. I heard her trust. I heard her freedom.

And in that moment, standing in that shallow end, holding a woman I had just met, whispering words I didn't even plan to say, I knew.

I knew this was what I was supposed to do with my life.

SECTION IV: The Revelation

That moment in the pool wasn't just about helping someone experience water. It was about dignity and trust. It was about looking at another human being and saying, "I see you as a whole person, and I will not let fear stop me from helping you experience joy."

It was about refusing to let barriers determine what was possible, whether those barriers were physical like stairs and ramps, or human like fear and uncertainty. And it was about one simple promise: I got you. Not "I'll try." Not "Maybe." Not "If it's convenient." Just that simple truth. I got you.

That day, I learned something that has guided every decision I've made in this field. People don't need you to have all the answers. They need you to show up. They need you to say yes when others say no. They need you to believe in their possibility when the world tells them it's too complicated, too expensive, too risky. They need you to whisper "I got you" and mean it.

SECTION V: From the Pool to the Page

Thirty-eight years later, I am still saying it.

I'm saying it to every person who has been told their independence is impossible.

I'm saying it to every provider who feels trapped by outdated systems.

I'm saying it to every state director who knows we need to change but doesn't know where to start.

I'm saying it to every DSP who is exhausted, underpaid, and wondering if this work still matters.

I'm saying it to every family who is terrified of what happens when they can no longer provide care.

I'm saying it to my grandmother's memory, the woman who left everything she knew so that I could have options.

And I'm saying it to the future, the one we are building right now, together.

I got you.

Just relax.

I got you.

Nothing is going to happen to you that we can't handle together.

SECTION VI: The BBC Director Was Right

A few years ago, I had the opportunity to work with a team from the BBC. They were filming a documentary, a mini-series about the human side of technology and how it was changing lives. They had heard about the work my team and I were doing with enabling technology, and they wanted to capture it on film. They wanted to show how we were using technology to help someone live more independently, to live their best life.

We spent weeks together. Cameras following us. Interviews. The whole production experience. And during that time, something happened that none of us expected.

The technology we had implemented for the woman we were supporting revealed some health concerns that she wasn't even aware of. She was someone who could articulate, someone who could speak for herself and tell you how she was feeling. But the technology saw something she couldn't feel yet. The data was showing patterns that indicated a problem before her body gave her any warning signs.

Because of that early detection, we were able to get her to appropriate medical care. We were able to intervene before a crisis became a tragedy. Her life didn't just stabilize. It improved. That's the power of what we were building, and the BBC captured it happening in real time.

When the filming wrapped, I sat down with the director for a final conversation. I expected him to talk about the footage, the editing process, when the documentary might air. Instead, he looked at me and said something I didn't fully process until I started writing this book.

He told me that I didn't need a documentary mini-series. He said I needed a Star Wars. A forever story to be told. He said I needed to write a book, speak on large platforms, host events at universities. He said the story I was living in real life was so compelling and so amazing that everybody needed to hear it.

And then he paused and made sure I understood what he meant. He said he wasn't saying this to boost my head. This wasn't about me. It was about how lives get exposed to be as beautiful and as authentic as they possibly can, because there are people advocating for them to live that beautiful life.

He was right.

This isn't about me. It's about the woman in the pool who finally got to feel weightless. It's about my grandmother who left her home so I could have choices. It's about the man with COPD who got to keep living independently because technology detected a stroke he didn't even know he was having. It's about the young woman from Guatemala who reconnected with her culture through a screen and reclaimed the identity adoption had taken from her. It's about every person who has been told that safety and freedom are opposites, when the truth is they are partners.

This is about all of us. And this story, this movement, needs a lifetime of telling.

SECTION VI-B: The Wedding He Never Imagined

I need to tell you one more story.

Because this one sits somewhere deep in my subconscious, right next to the story of my grandparents leaving Barnwell, South Carolina for New York. They were born into limitations, division, small windows of hope, and yet their sacrifice turned into me sitting here, writing this book, telling you about dreams.

This story is about what becomes possible when a team sees the dream instead of the barrier.

I was working for a very large provider in New York, a national organization that worked with people who had severe physical, medical, and developmental disabilities. I was in an ICF at the time, a large one. Twelve people living in one setting. Every person had severe, compounding conditions, medical, physical, developmental, cognitive.

But there were no limitations on hope.

There were no limitations on dreams.

And I attribute so much of who I am today to what I experienced working in that environment. Everything is possible. *Everything.*

Among the twelve people living there, three of them were siblings, part of a large, loving Colombian family that had migrated to the United States. All three were born with a similar genetic condition, layered with medical, cognitive, and developmental disabilities. All three had conditions that affected their muscular and skeletal function. All three were nonverbal, meaning they didn't use verbal words to speak, although they communicated beautifully. They used spelling boards, keyboards on their lap trays, pointing to letters one by one while we repeated them aloud.

They understood both English and Spanish.

All three were on G-tube feeding.

All three needed total care, bathing, toileting, medical support.

All three were in custom wheelchairs. Serious custom wheelchairs. The kind that looked like Cadillacs, built by occupational therapists and physical therapists who understood that dignity includes how you move through the world.

And all three had dreams.

The oldest of the siblings had a dream that changed everything.

She wanted to date.

And then she wanted to marry.

Now, imagine sitting in an ISP meeting, and this woman is communicating through finger spelling, pointing to letters on a laminated keyboard attached to her lap tray, one letter at a time, while we repeat each letter out loud. A single sentence could take ten minutes. A full story could take hours.

But she had something to say.

She had met a man at her day program. He had physical disabilities too, used a rolling walker, had limited use of his hands, but he could speak with verbal words. And she wanted to date him.

So we planned.

We prepared.

We thought through every detail.

She was on a pureed diet, no liquids by mouth, only certain textures of food. So when they went to a local diner for their first date, we brought a blender. Just in case the restaurant couldn't accommodate her needs.

We helped her get ready. Victoria's Secret body lotions, she loved the way they smelled. Makeup. She wanted to feel beautiful. She wanted to feel like a woman going on a date. Because that's exactly what she was.

And we prepared conversation cards, pre-written statements she could point to so the conversation could flow naturally, so she wouldn't have to spell every word while he waited.

We thought of everything.

But we were nervous about her father.

He was a traditional Colombian father. The patriarch. The one whose blessing would matter most. And we weren't sure how he would respond to his daughter, this daughter, with all her medical needs and physical dependencies, wanting to date. Wanting romance. Wanting love.

He was at the meeting. He understood everything she said.

And when he finally spoke, his voice broke.

"I don't even know what to say. I don't even know what to do. I have... I have problems understanding that the other girls, the other siblings, were going to go on dates. But this child..."

He paused. Caught himself.

"She's an adult. I know. But I never imagined I would be at this table talking about this with her."

He agreed to support it. He just didn't want all the details.

Like most parents.

The relationship lasted.

The dates continued.

The connection deepened.

And then one day, the man decided he was going to propose.

He needed our help. He wanted to do it right. He wanted to ask her father for her hand in marriage, the traditional way, the respectful way, the way that would honor her family's culture.

So we rehearsed.

We practiced what he would say. We helped him learn to pronounce words clearly, he had difficulty articulating certain sounds even in English. We brought a gift for the family, a fruit arrangement. And we helped him learn one phrase in Spanish.

Hola.

Just that one word. But he wanted to say it. He wanted to honor them.

The day came.

We went to the family's home. The whole family was there, siblings, parents, extended relatives. A large, loving Colombian family gathered to witness something none of them had ever expected.

He spoke. Slowly. Carefully. With all the dignity and earnestness a man in love can carry.

And then he tried to get on his knee.

But he couldn't.

His physical disability wouldn't allow it. His body couldn't bend that way. If he tried to kneel, he would end up laying on the floor.

So that's what he did.

He laid himself down. He looked up at her father. He held the ring in his hand.

And he asked for her hand in marriage.

Everyone was crying.

Every single person in that room.

The staff. The family. The siblings. Me.

We were all weeping.

Because we were witnessing something sacred. Something that too many people assumed would never happen for someone like her. Something the world had written off as impossible.

The father said yes.

But the story doesn't end there.

The father was a tailor. A seamstress by trade.

And he made his daughter's wedding dress.

Not just any dress.

He designed it. He tailored it. He retrofitted it so that the train would drape beautifully around her custom wheelchair. So that when people saw her rolling down that aisle, they wouldn't see limitations.

They would see a bride.

He sat crying while he worked, he told us later.

Because he never imagined, never in his life imagined, that he would be able to walk this daughter down the aisle.

And yet here he was.

Because a team saw the dream instead of the barrier.

Because an organization believed that everything is possible.

Because love doesn't ask for permission from disability.

They got married.

They've been in marital bliss ever since.

And I carry that story with me everywhere I go. Because it proves what I've always believed:

Barriers are structures we create in our minds.

And if we can break them in our minds, everything is possible.

Everything.

SECTION VII: What Happens Next

So here we are.

You've read this book.

You know the stories.

You know the frameworks.

You know the history.

You know the possibilities.

Now what?

Here's what I need you to understand:

This is not the end of the conversation.

This is the beginning.

This book is not meant to give you every answer. It's meant to show you that answers exist, and that we can build them together.

If you're a state director reading this, you now know that the federal intent has supported technology for nearly 50 years. You know that innovation is not a luxury, it is a responsibility. And you know that the barriers are not in the regulations. They are in our willingness to imagine something different.

If you're a provider CEO, you now know that enabling technology is not about replacing staff. It's about empowering them. It's about giving your workforce the tools to do meaningful work instead of just occupying shifts. It's about sustainability, dignity, and the future of care.

If you're a DSP, you now know that your voice matters. That technology can protect you from investigative leave for things that weren't your fault. That you deserve to feel safe, supported, and valued in this work.

If you're a family member, you now know that there are options beyond what the system has traditionally offered. That independence and safety are not opposites. That your loved one deserves the dignity of choice.

If you're a person with a disability or a senior trying to age in place, you now know that the tools exist. That the future can be designed for you. Not around you, but *for you.*

And if you're an innovator, a policymaker, a thought leader, or someone who just finished this book and thought, "*We have to do something,*" then you are exactly who this movement needs.

SECTION VIII: Your Next Three Steps

I'm not going to leave you hanging.

Here's what you do next:

Step 1: Decide What You Believe

Do you believe that people deserve independence?

Do you believe that technology can support freedom without stealing dignity?

Do you believe that the systems we built in 1988 are not sufficient for 2025?

If the answer is yes, then you're already part of this movement.

Step 2: Take One Action This Week

Just one.

- If you're a leader: Start a conversation about enabling technology at your next team meeting.

- If you're a policymaker: Review your state's Medicaid waiver language and look for opportunities to support innovation.

- If you're a provider: Reach out to someone who is already doing this work and ask how they started.

- If you're a family: Ask your loved one what independence means to them, and listen without assuming you know the answer.

- If you're a person receiving support: Tell someone what you want. Not what you think is possible, but what you *want.*

One action. This week.

Step 3: Connect With the Movement

You are not alone in this.

There are providers across the country who are building enabling technology environments. There are states that are rewriting their service models. There are families who are advocating for their loved ones to have the same freedoms everyone else takes for granted. There are DSPs who are learning how to use technology to make their jobs more meaningful. And there is a growing community of people who refuse to go back to 1988.

Visit www.vistasupports.com to learn more about training, resources, and how to connect with this movement.

The future is not built by one person. It's built by all of us, together.

SECTION IX: The Vision for 2030

Let me paint you a picture of what I see when I close my eyes and imagine the future we're building.

It's 2030.

A young man with a developmental disability wakes up in his own apartment. Not a group home. Not an institution. Not his parents' house because "there are no other options."

His apartment.

He wakes up to music he chose, at a time he set, in a bed he picked out himself.

His smart home knows his routine. The lights come on gradually. The coffee pot starts brewing. His medication reminder chimes softly, not intrusively, but gently, because the system knows he takes his meds better when he's had his coffee first.

He checks his tablet. His remote support team sent him a message: "Good morning! Your mom's birthday is next week, do you want help ordering flowers?"

He smiles. He does.

He gets ready for his day. He has a job he's good at. He has friends he chose. He has a life that looks like *his life*. Not a care plan someone else wrote for him.

If he needs help, it's there. Not hovering. Not intrusive. Just there, like a safety net you trust but rarely see.

Technology didn't replace the people in his life.

It gave him room to breathe.

And across town, an 80-year-old woman sits in the home she's lived in for 40 years. The home where she raised her children. The home where her husband passed. The home that smells like her, sounds like her, feels like her.

She's aging in place.

Not because she has unlimited money.

Not because she has family available 24/7.

But because the system finally caught up to what she always knew was possible.

Her health is monitored. Her safety is supported. Her independence is protected.

And when her granddaughter calls on video to say, "Grandma, I'm coming to visit next week," she doesn't have to worry about whether someone will be there to let her in.

Because she can see who's at the door.

Because she can unlock it herself.

Because technology gave her back control.

This is the future I see.

A future where:

- Independence is the default, not the exception.

- Safety and freedom are partners, not enemies.

- Culture is honored, not erased.

- Technology serves humanity, not the other way around.

- People are trusted to live their own lives.

This is the future we're building.

And you're part of it.

SECTION X: But God

Before I close this book, I need to tell you something personal.

Something I don't talk about often.

Something that almost broke me.

I've told you stories throughout this book about "catching heck" for pushing innovation. About agencies questioning my methods. About having to justify, rewrite plans, attend extra meetings, explain myself over and over again.

That's not what I'm talking about now.

That kind of resistance? I can handle that. I'll teach. I'll educate. I'll explain. I'll win people over. I love doing that. And at the end of the day, somebody is still going to live their best life. So I don't care how many meetings you make me sit through.

But there's a different kind of resistance.

A darker kind.

The kind that doesn't just question your methods, it tries to crush your spirit.

I'm a spiritual person. I believe in light and dark. Good and evil. Heaven and hell. If you're into Star Wars, you know what I mean, the saber either comes to you or it doesn't. And when the resistance you're facing comes from a dark spirit, it's harder to fight. Because it's not tangible. It's not a policy you can change or a regulation you can cite. It's something happening in the spiritual realm.

And I faced it.

There was a season in my life when I was winning.

Not winning for myself, winning for the movement.

I was gaining opportunities to speak on larger platforms. Governments were calling me. Media was paying attention. I was entering spaces that our field had never been invited into before. And everywhere I went, I brought my team with me. I branded them. I lifted them. I made sure everyone knew this wasn't just me. This was US.

I was advancing innovation. Advancing services. Advancing the very mission we were supposed to be building together.

And I was told to stop.

Not by regulators. Not by families. Not by the people I supported.

By people in my own house.

I was told that nobody wanted to hear from me. That nobody wanted to hear the stories I had to tell. That my speaking was making others feel intimidated. That I talked too much. That I should apologize, before I even opened my mouth, for not knowing how to be brief.

I was told to fade to the back so others could shine.

Now, let me be clear: I have spent my entire career breaking down barriers so that others CAN shine. That's what I do. That's my purpose. I lay bricks underneath people's feet so they can stand taller.

But what I was being told wasn't about lifting others up.

It was about shrinking me down.

It was about the fact that I had grown, in their minds, too big for what they had imagined me to be.

And that broke something in me.

I can't tell you how many people I've trained who now hold major positions. Directors. Executives. Business owners. Doctorates. People I hired, mentored, poured into. I'm not saying I'm the only reason they succeeded, but I know I laid a few bricks underneath their feet.

And I never brought that up. Not once. Until now.

Because that's not why I do this work.

I do this work because somebody poured into me first.

Cindi Staib. Yvette Figueroa. Melissa Arenas-Dewitt. Nurse Jane. These are foundational names. Women who gave me free range to expand my talents. Women who taught me well. Women who showed me what it looked like to pour out so that others could rise.

And Beth Mount. Beth gave me my first stage. She invited me to accompany her and share my story of the married couple, the woman from the Colombian family and her husband, and how we helped them live their best lives together. That speaking opportunity opened doors I didn't even know existed. Beth saw something in me and gave me a platform to share it.

Everything I've done in this field, every innovation, every framework, every life changed, came from what these people planted in me at the very beginning. It would be a disservice not to continue pouring out.

My grandmother used to say: "We ain't gonna be for everybody. But we for somebody."

I may not be your cup of tea. But I'm somebody's champagne.

There was a season when I faced resistance. Not the kind that comes from regulators questioning your methods or agencies wanting more documentation. That kind of resistance I can handle. I'll teach, I'll educate, I'll explain. At the end of the day, somebody is still going to live their best life.

This was a different kind of resistance. The kind that tried to make me smaller. The kind that suggested my gifts were too much, that I should fade to the back, that I should apologize for the very thing I was put on this earth to do.

And in that season, I had to hold onto what I knew to be true. My voice is not an accident. It's an assignment. It is my purpose to use whatever room I enter to bring along people who would not have had the ability to enter that space themselves. It is my calling to speak on behalf of those who may not have a voice. I lend my voice to people who need it.

That's not arrogance. That's obedience to what I was created for.

I remember being in Chicago O'Hare airport. Anybody who knows that airport knows it's like four cities in one building. I was running from one gate to another, looking ratchet, out of breath, and my phone rings.

A government entity needed me to get on a call. Right then. To help explain enabling technology to federal officials. To help move regulations forward that would allow more people to use technology to live independently.

I didn't think twice. I found a corner. I got on the call. I did what I do.

And we moved something forward that day. Afterward, they called me "clutch."

I never thought about that moment again until right now. Because that's not why I do it. I don't do it for the title or the recognition. I do it because if my God-given talent can be utilized, I need to use it. Period.

So when I faced that season of resistance, I had a choice. I could shrink. Or I could keep speaking.

I chose to keep speaking.

Not out of spite. Not out of bitterness. Out of faith.

My faith tells me that all I need is faith the size of a mustard seed. You know how small that is? I have a bottle in my spice cabinet. Just one of those tiny seeds, and with that little bit of faith, I can tell a mountain to move.

That means I can speak movement into the universe.

I can speak.

So I speak.

And here I am.

Writing this book.

Giving flowers where they belong.

Celebrating innovation.

Pushing the movement forward.

Being The Voice of Enabling Technology™.

Building a YouTube channel where all I do is talk and motivate people to look past their barriers and find their best, healthy, and free selves.

The very thing that dark spirit tried to take out of me?

It's now the very thing that pushes me forward.

But God.

They tried to silence me.

But God.

They told me to apologize for my gifts.

But God.

They said nobody wanted to hear from me.

But God.

Here I am.

And here you are, reading these words.

But God.

If you're reading this and you've ever been told you're too much, too loud, too passionate, too ambitious, too visible, I need you to hear me:

Don't you dare shrink.

Don't you dare apologize for the gifts God gave you.

Don't you dare fade to the back because someone else is uncomfortable with your light.

You may not be everybody's cup of tea.

But you are somebody's champagne.

And the world needs what you carry.

But God.

CLOSING: I'm Still in That Pool

Thirty-eight years later, I am still that 14-year-old girl standing in the shallow end of a YMCA pool.

I'm still whispering the same words.

I got you.

Just relax.

I got you.

Everything is going to be okay.

But now, I'm not just saying it to one person.

I'm saying it to an entire field.

I'm saying it to every person who has been told their dream is too expensive, too complicated, too risky.

I'm saying it to every provider who feels trapped by systems that don't make sense anymore.

I'm saying it to every state leader who knows we need to change but doesn't know where to start.

I'm saying it to my grandmother's spirit, the woman who left her home so that I could dream bigger.

And I'm saying it to you.

Because this work, this movement, this future we're building together, it's not about having all the answers.

It's about showing up.

It's about saying yes when others say no.

It's about refusing to let fear, tradition, or outdated systems determine what's possible.

It's about believing that people deserve more than survival.

They deserve to thrive.

They deserve to be seen.

They deserve to be trusted.

They deserve to be free.

And if we build this right, if we center humanity, honor culture, and use technology as the tool it was always meant to be, then the future we create will be one we're all proud to grow old in.

So here's my final ask:

Don't just read this book and put it on a shelf.

Don't just nod and say, "That was nice."

Don't just agree and then go back to the way things were.

Do something.

One thing.

This week.

And then do another thing next week.

And another the week after that.

Because the future doesn't wait for us to get comfortable.

The future happens because we decide to build it.

And I'm building it.

With or without permission.

With or without funding.

With or without applause.

Because thirty-eight years ago, I stood in a pool and made a promise to a woman I had just met.

I got you.

And I've been keeping that promise ever since.

Now I'm making that same promise to you.

I got you.

We got this.

Let's build the future together.

CHAPTER 13: WHAT COMES NEXT: A Call to Build Together

This book is a starting point, not a finish line.

I want to be honest with you about what these pages contain and what they don't. I've given you frameworks that took me nearly four decades to develop. I've given you stories that I hope moved you and made you think differently about what's possible. I've given you data that proves this work can be done at scale. I've given you a vision for what the future of care could look like if we had the courage to build it.

But a book can only do so much. The real work happens after you close these pages.

So let me speak directly to each of you, because I know who's reading this and I know what you're thinking.

To the families who picked up this book because you're exhausted and you're looking for answers, I want you to know that your instincts are right. When you feel like the system isn't working for your loved one, you're not imagining it. When you feel like there should be more options, more dignity, more freedom, you're not being unreasonable. You're being human. And you deserve a system that honors that humanity. Take the Seven Freedoms from Chapter 5 and bring them to your next ISP meeting. Ask your provider why these aren't being addressed. Ask your state why these aren't in the waiver. You have more power than you think, and your voice matters more than you know. Don't let anyone tell you that what you're asking for is too much. It's not too much. It's the bare minimum of what your loved one deserves.

To the state directors and policymakers who read the chapters on funding and regulations, I know what you're up against. I know the budget constraints. I know the political pressures. I know that innovation feels risky when your name is attached to every decision. But I also know that you got into this work because you believed you could make a difference. Somewhere along the way, the system may have convinced you that the best you can do is maintain what already exists. I'm here to tell you that's not true. The states that are leading right now, the ones implementing Technology First policies and rewriting their waiver language, they're not doing it because they have more resources than you. They're doing it because they decided that the status quo wasn't acceptable anymore. You can make that same decision. And when you do, reach out. Let's share what's working. Let's build a network of states that are willing to show others what's possible. The field needs your leadership, and the people you serve need you to be brave.

To the CEOs and agency leaders who are sitting with this book wondering if transformation is really possible for your organization, I see you. I know the weight you carry. I know you're trying to balance mission and margin, quality and compliance, innovation and stability. I know your board is cautious and your staff are tired and your margins are thin. But I also know that you didn't build your organization to maintain the status quo. You built it to serve people well. And the truth is, the old model is breaking whether you transform or not. The workforce crisis isn't going away. The regulatory environment is shifting. The expectations of the people you serve are evolving. You can either lead that change or be swept up by it. I'd rather see you lead. Start small. Pick one home. Pick one program. Build your proof of concept. Show your board what's possible. And when you're ready to scale, the roadmap is in Chapter 11.

To my fellow innovators. And yes, I'm talking to those of you who might see me as competition. I want to say something that might surprise you. I'm not interested in competing with you. The field is too big and the need is too great for us to be fighting over territory. What I am interested in is collaboration. We Are Team Innovation, and I mean that literally. WATI is not just a brand. It's an invitation. If you're doing good work in this space, if you're building solutions that honor people's dignity and expand their freedom, then we're on the same team. Let's share what we're learning. Let's refer to each other when our expertise doesn't fit. Let's build something together that none of us could build alone. The old mindset of scarcity and competition belongs to the old system. We're building something new, and there's room for all of us at the table.

I know this because I've lived it.

I am a proud graduate of the ANCOR Leadership Academy. Class of 2022. We started at the beginning of the pandemic in 2020, when everything was falling apart and we were all trying to figure out how to hold it together. I remember logging into those virtual sessions thinking

I didn't have time for this, that I should be putting out fires back at my agency. But something happened in that space that I didn't expect. When you put purpose-driven leaders in a room together, even a virtual one, something shifts. You stop managing crises long enough to remember why you started this work in the first place. You get to dream out loud with people who understand what you're up against. You get refreshed. There's a scripture that says, "He who refreshes others will himself be refreshed." That's what the Leadership Academy did for me. And that's why I serve on the ANCOR Foundation Board now. The Academy is its star project, and I believe in what it's building. We need leaders who understand that the future is transforming the traditional. Not abandoning it. Transforming it. And that takes intentional development, not just survival.

As President of the DC Coalition of Disability Service Providers, I've learned something else about building together. For over two decades, I've been a participating member on many different levels. Sometimes as part of the body, sometimes as a committee chair, sometimes as a board member. And what I've come to understand is that providers don't have to compete for scraps. We can build together. That's why the Coalition agreed to host an Enabling Technology Community of Practice. Because technology cannot be an afterthought. Innovation cannot be something we talk about at one conference a year and then forget when we get back to our desks. It has to be woven into how we operate, how we train, how we advocate.

And I tell our members all the time: bump the now. If you in the now, you already late. You got to stay within the future.

Let me explain what I mean by that.

For too long, we've been using a parking lot analogy. Like we're all just trying to find a space, park our agencies somewhere stable, and hope we don't get towed. But the parking lot analogy is dead. We have to see this as a driveway now. A long driveway. And the future is already standing at the end of it, watching to see who's coming. The question is: does the future see you pulling up? Can it say, "Oh, I see Provider A coming down the lane. I see Provider B right behind them. Let me make space"? Or are you still in the parking lot? Or worse, you haven't even left your building yet? That's the question every provider needs to answer. And as a coalition, our job is to make sure our members are on the driveway, visible, moving, ready for what's coming. Because something is always coming.

You know what's coming right now? A whole new understanding of what community even means.

Think about it. Back in 1971, when the ICF movement started, we were fighting to get people out of institutions. Physical institutions. Big campuses where people with disabilities were separated from society, warehoused, forgotten. The de-institutionalization movement said no. These are human beings, and they deserve to live in the community. That was a righteous fight, and it changed where people lived. But here's what that movement didn't fully change: how we support people once they got there.

And now, decades later, we're facing a new version of the same problem. Because nobody is living in the physical community at 100 percent anymore. None of us are. We all use social media. We all use LinkedIn and Facebook and group chats and online platforms. We find out about events in a digital space and then show up in a physical space. The digital community is where connection happens first now. It's where information flows. It's where people build relationships and find opportunities and stay in touch with the people they love.

So if people with disabilities and seniors aging in place are not included in the digital community, then where are they? They're in a new kind of institution. Not a building this time. An exclusion. A separation that's just as real as those old campuses, except now it's invisible. You can live in an apartment in the middle of a city and still be institutionalized if no one taught you how to use a smartphone. You can have your own bedroom and still be cut off from the world if the people supporting you don't understand why TikTok matters to a 25-year-old or why your grandmother wants to FaceTime her great-grandchildren.

This is the new movement. We're not just moving people from institutions to physical communities anymore. We're moving people from physical-only existence into a hybrid reality where they can participate fully. Online and offline. Digital and in-person. Connected in every way that matters. And if that's not an idea worth spreading, I don't know what is. This message belongs on every stage that will have it. From provider conferences to TEDx stages to the rooms where policy gets made. Because this is not just about technology. This is about freedom. This is about making sure the next generation doesn't inherit a system that accidentally excluded an entire population from the way the world actually works now.

I didn't come to this understanding sitting in an office. I came to it by being present in rooms where I wasn't always sure I belonged.

I'm a founding member of Baddies in Tech. And let me tell you something. When I walk into that space and put on that letterman jacket, it comes with a whole different kind of flex. Because I'm not a coder. I'm not IT. I'm a human services provider who uses tech in a very intentional way to transform traditional services into the future of care. But here's the thing. I learned my first computer commands on one of the early Macintosh computers back in elementary school. District 28, Queens, New York City public schools. Shout out. We were one of the first classrooms to get those machines in our lab, and I learned DOS commands before I learned how to type a proper essay. Front slash, back slash, how to tell a computer what to do. So when people are talking about prompting AI agents now, I understand the language because I've been speaking it since I was a child. I just didn't know that's what it was called.

Full circle.

And now I get to build AI agents for myself, teach agencies how to prompt technology for better outcomes, and sit in rooms with brilliant coders and engineers as a bridge. Because that's my role in Baddies in Tech. I'm not writing the code. I'm connecting two worlds that might never have met each other otherwise. I'm telling those super smart developers that there's a whole population of people with disabilities and seniors who need what they're building, and here's how to build it right. I'm representing for every woman of color who was in technology spaces but never got to flex. They were there. And now we're here. And when those young women coming up behind us see someone who looks like them holding space in tech, that matters. Representation always matters.

When I was invited to join the Techquity Board, I was already deep into writing this book. A board called Techquity. A book called Tech Equity. You can't tell me that was coincidence. That was confirmation. That was God saying, "Keep going. The seat was already prepared for you." And the work that board is doing, asking hard questions about whether technology actually does what it claims to do for people with disabilities, that's advocacy at a level I hadn't seen before. We're not just asking if the device works. We're asking if it works for this person, in this context, in a way that honors their dignity. That's a different question.

And it's the right one.

And then there's The Gathering Spot. I'm a founding member here in DC. Second or third cohort, I lose track. But what I don't lose track of is why that space matters to me. It's about culture and representation and bringing the talents of the village together. I think about the biblical image of people gathering in the town center, everyone bringing their goods and their gifts so that no one goes without. That's what TGS represents to me. It's where I met Cordelia Crenshaw, who leads Acts of Random Kindness, mentoring young women in foster care who are building their futures against odds that would break most people. Through that connection, I get to pour into the next generation. I get to teach them about technology and advocacy and how a woman of color carries herself and doesn't shrink. I am a childless mother. The auntie of all aunties. And when those young women see me from across the room and come running to give me a hug, that's not networking. That's legacy. That's making sure the future is bright because I can see the talent that's going into it.

I share all of this because I want you to understand that building together isn't just a slogan for me. It's how I move through the world. Every board seat, every membership, every mentorship feeds into the same mission.

And I'll tell you one more story that brought it home for me.

I'm a proud member of the DC Chamber of Commerce and the Women in Business Committee. And I'll be honest. Sometimes in those rooms, I wonder if what I do matters on the same level as everyone else at the table. You've got women running hospital networks across a tri-state area. Women building developments that change a city's skyline. And then there's me, talking about helping people with disabilities use technology to live their best lives. It can feel small if you let it.

But one day, I decided to stop shrinking. I told my whole story. How I started at fourteen years old, how I became a program director trying to figure out how to keep people engaged and staff fulfilled, how I discovered that technology was the answer, and how I went from helping one person at a time to realizing that every provider could benefit from what I was learning. I told them about Vista Supports. How I didn't just want to be a provider, I wanted to build up providers. If I'm sitting on all this knowledge and all this advocacy, why would I keep it to myself? Providers support people. Vista Supports supports providers. That's the model. That's the mission.

And when I finished talking, something happened that I didn't expect. These women, the hospital network administrators, the developers, the executives with jobs way bigger than mine, they leaned in. One of them said, "I've never heard about this from this perspective." Another one said, "My elderly parents need this. Can you help me?" And in that moment, I understood something I want every reader of this book to understand: if you're not at the table, the table doesn't hear what you have to offer. And if you shrink when you get there, you rob someone of the solution they didn't know they needed.

That's what building together looks like. It's showing up. It's sharing even when you're not sure anyone cares. It's being the bridge between worlds that don't know they need each other yet.

To the technology vendors and manufacturers who are reading this wondering if there's a market opportunity here, let me be direct with you. There is. But not the way you might be thinking about it. The disability and aging services field is not a market to be exploited. It's a community to be served. And the difference between those two approaches is everything. If you come in trying to sell solutions that weren't designed with this population in mind, you will fail. The Dean Martin Problem will catch you every time. Generic doesn't work here. But if you come in willing to listen, willing to co-design, willing to build WITH the community instead of FOR the community, then we need you. We need your engineering talent. We need your manufacturing capacity. We need your distribution networks. What we don't need is another tech company that treats disabled people and aging adults as an afterthought. Come correct, or don't come at all. And to my friends at CTA, when you see me at CES, let's have that conversation. I'll be the one talking about enabling technology like it's a civil rights issue. Because it is.

To the families of seniors and disabled veterans who found their way to this book, I want you to know that you're not forgotten. Much of what I've written focuses on the IDD and DD systems because that's where I've spent my career, but the principles are universal. Your father who served this country deserves to age with dignity in his own home. Your mother who worked her whole life deserves technology that supports her independence without making her feel surveilled. The frameworks in this book apply to you too. The Seven Freedoms don't care what system you're navigating. Safety, freedom, and connection matter whether you're dealing with Medicaid waivers or VA benefits or Medicare or private insurance. Take what's useful from these pages and adapt it to your situation. And push me to do more. I hear you. The veteran-specific guidance and the Medicare-specific applications are future work that needs to happen, and your voice will help make sure it does.

To CMS and the federal policymakers who shape the rules we all operate under, I want to acknowledge something. I've been critical in this book about the 1988 framework and the pace of regulatory change. But I also want to be clear that I understand the complexity of what you're managing. You're not the enemy. You're the guardrails that protect people from exploitation and abuse. That matters. What I'm asking for is not deregulation. What I'm asking for is evolution. The intent of the original regulations was person-centered care and active treatment and community integration. That intent was right. But the implementation tools have to evolve as technology evolves and as our understanding of what's possible evolves. I know you're watching the field. I know you're tracking the innovation happening in states that are pushing the envelope. I'm asking you to create pathways for that innovation to spread. Not by looking the other way, but by actively shaping guidance that makes it easier for good actors to do good work. The field needs your partnership in this.

Now let me tell you what comes next for me and for this movement.

This book identified gaps that still need to be filled, and I'm committed to filling them. The state-by-state case studies that show exactly how Tennessee or Maryland wrote their waiver language, that's future work that needs to happen. The companion workbook that gives families and frontline workers a practical tool they can use without reading three hundred pages, that's coming. The academic validation that takes these frameworks from practitioner wisdom to peer-reviewed research, I'm actively seeking university partnerships to make that happen. The AI-enabled virtual assistant that solves the Dean Martin Problem and supports QIDPs and families with context-specific guidance, that's what I'm building through House of CINO right now.

And WATI, We Are Team Innovation, is where all of this comes together. Not the Institute, which stays focused on certifications and professional development with its own ethics and standards. I'm talking about WATI the movement. The community. The big tent where everyone who believes in this vision can connect and collaborate and push each other forward. If you read this book and you felt something, if you recognized yourself in these pages, if you're ready to be part of building something different, then WATI is your home. Join us.

The future of enabling technology will not be built by any one person or any one organization. It will be built by a community of people who refuse to accept that the current system is the best we can do. People who believe that technology should expand freedom, not restrict it. People who understand that dignity is not a privilege to be earned but a right to be protected. People who are willing to do the hard work of transformation even when it's uncomfortable and uncertain and slow.

That's who this book was written for.

That's who WATI is building for.

That's who I've been fighting for since I was fourteen years old standing in that pool.

So here's my final invitation to you. Don't just read this book and put it on a shelf. Do something with it. Share it with someone who needs to hear this message. Bring it to a meeting and challenge the people in the room to think differently. Use the frameworks to advocate for what you or your loved one deserves. Reach out and tell me what you're building. Join the movement.

We are Team Innovation.

And together, we're going to build something that sets people free.

WHAT I'M BUILDING

Throughout this book, I've described a problem that no generic technology can solve.

I call it the Dean Martin Problem, and I told you about it in Chapter 4.

When a person with a developmental disability says "Dean Martin" and means "I'm ready for bed," no algorithm trained on general population data will understand. When cultural nuance, personal history, and individual communication patterns determine what words actually mean, technology built for the masses will always fail the margins.

This is exactly the problem I'm working to solve.

I am actively developing AI-enabled virtual assistance designed specifically for the IDD and DD field through House of CINO, my digital products company. Not a generic chatbot. Not a one-size-fits-all solution borrowed from another industry. An intelligent system trained on the Enabled Life Model to interpret and support individual, cultural, and personal communication. Something that can help providers, DSPs, families, and people receiving services navigate the complexity of this work with support that actually understands the context.

The QIDP role, the Qualified Intellectual Disabilities Professional, is one of the most under-resourced positions in our entire system, and this AI assistant is designed to support that role as well. To help interpret regulations and translate them into practical guidance. To support plan development that is both compliant AND person-centered. To give the people responsible for ensuring quality outcomes the tools they need to actually achieve those outcomes.

The Administration for Community Living recently launched the Caregiver AI Competition, recognizing that AI can play a role in supporting caregivers and improving outcomes. That federal recognition validates what I've known for years: we need intelligent systems designed for our field, by people who understand our field.

The future of enabling technology will not come from Silicon Valley. It will come from the people who have been doing this work for decades, who understand that technology is only as good as the humanity behind it.

The WATI Institute is where professionals come to develop the real skills that will advance our traditional services into a future-ready state. It combines theory, translates traditional service concepts, and focuses on practical application. Participants will be certified at multiple levels, because this work requires different depths of expertise depending on your role. This is how we solve the workforce crisis: not by hoping more people show up, but by equipping the people we have with skills that make them more effective.

That's what I'm building.

And now that you've read this book, you're part of the vision too.

RESOURCES & NEXT STEPS

For all resources, community access, and to join the movement:

TechEquityBook.com

For Speaking Engagements, Consulting, or State-Level Support:

links.pmbofficial.com

The Voice of Enabling Technology™

"I got you. Just relax. I got you. Everything is going to be okay."

GLOSSARY OF TERMS

The language we use shapes how we think. These definitions reflect a humanity-centered approach to enabling technology. When the field uses these terms, they should mean what's written here.

Active Treatment

A regulatory requirement in ICF/IID settings that mandates continuous, aggressive, and consistent implementation of specialized and generic training, treatment, health services, and related services. Active treatment is designed to help individuals function with as much self-determination and independence as possible.

Appendix K

A provision that allows states to request emergency amendments to their HCBS waivers. During the COVID-19 pandemic, Appendix K waivers enabled flexibilities including remote service delivery, modified staffing requirements, and companion care arrangements that demonstrated the viability of alternative service models.

Assistive Technology (AT)

Any device, software, or system that empowers individuals to perform tasks, control their environment, and actively influence their own lives. Ranging from simple daily living aids to advanced digital platforms, AT provides the practical means for a person to communicate choices, complete tasks, and navigate the world with autonomy. It is the toolset that bridges the gap between intent and action. In the Ritmo Framework™, AT represents The Beat: the individual instrument in a person's Soundtrack of Life.

CINO VISTA Consulting LLC

A strategic consulting firm founded by Precious "Preciosa" Myers-Brown that helps small IDD/DD agencies build, digitize, and grow by developing innovation foundations. CINO VISTA combines strategic guidance with scalable tools and systems, empowering providers to move from paper-heavy and invisible to tech-enabled and thriving.

Cultural Alignment

The practice of ensuring technology, services, and supports reflect and respect an individual's culture, language, identity, values, history, and community traditions. Technology that is not culturally aligned will be rejected or underutilized.

CMS (Centers for Medicare & Medicaid Services)

The federal agency that administers Medicare, Medicaid, and the Children's Health Insurance Program. CMS sets federal regulations and guidelines that states must follow when designing and implementing disability services, including HCBS waivers.

Companion Care

A service model where support is provided by individuals who may live with or spend extended time with a person receiving services, often in a more natural, less clinical relationship than traditional staffing models.

Dean Martin Problem

A term coined by Precious "Preciosa" Myers-Brown to describe the limitation of generic AI and technology when supporting people with disabilities. When a person says "Dean Martin" but means "I'm ready for bed," technology trained on general population data will fail to understand. This illustrates why enabling technology must be personalized to individual communication patterns and meanings.

Dean Martin Principle, The

A core tenet of Tech Equity asserting that technology must be programmed to honor personal meaning over universal definitions. Named after a specific case where generic AI would interpret "Dean Martin" as a celebrity to be discussed, but a personalized system understood it as a distress code rooted in the person's unique history. This principle establishes that Equity requires Context: a system that treats every user the same is not equitable; it is erasing their identity. True Tech Equity requires systems that act as Cultural Decoders, learning the unique language of the user's life.

Direct Support Professional (DSP)

A trained professional who provides direct care and support to individuals with disabilities. DSPs assist with daily living, community participation, health needs, and personal goals. They are the backbone of the care system and deserve to be treated as professionals.

Dignity of Risk

The principle that people have the right to take reasonable risks in pursuit of their goals, even if others might make different choices. True person-centered care honors dignity of risk rather than eliminating all possibility of failure.

Enabled Life

A life characterized by safety, freedom, and connection, supported by technology that enhances rather than restricts human experience. The goal of enabling technology is to help people live an enabled life on their own terms.

Enabled Life Model™

A 3x3 framework developed by Precious "Preciosa" Myers-Brown that defines what a dignified, empowered life looks like when technology supports human care. The three pillars are Safety (Predictive Support, Crisis Reduction, Health Insight), Freedom (Autonomy, Privacy, Personal Control), and Connection (Social Belonging, Cultural Alignment, Emotional Dignity).

Enabling Technology

Technology that supports independence, safety, communication, and community integration for people with disabilities and seniors. Unlike assistive technology, which addresses individual functions, enabling technology creates environments and systems that expand what's possible by connecting devices together. Examples include smart home devices, remote monitoring, sensors, and communication platforms working in concert. In the Ritmo Framework™, this represents The Groove: where devices begin to communicate, building relationships and learning each other's rhythms.

Enabling Technology Environment

A home or setting where multiple enabling technologies work together to support a person's independence, safety, and quality of life. This is not about individual devices but about an integrated, structured living space that responds to the person. In the Ritmo Framework™, this represents The Song: the composition where technology has become a committed household, with verses and choruses, patterns and progressions that play reliably day after day.

Enabling Technology Ecosystem

The comprehensive integration of assistive technology devices, smart supports, an enabling technology environment, hybrid staffing, and natural supports, all working together to address a person's Person-Centered Plan of care. In the Ritmo Framework™, this represents The Soundtrack and The Community: the full orchestra of technology and humans moving together to ensure the music never stops. A functioning ecosystem has RITMO. It has rhythm. The Beat (individual devices), The Groove (device interoperability), The Song (the structured environment), and The Soundtrack (the village of human support, policy, and backup systems) all move together in sync. When an ecosystem has RITMO, it functions like clockwork even if one or two entities are absent or missing. It evolves the more we engage it, becoming more refined and responsive over time. When an ecosystem loses RITMO, gaps appear, crises multiply, and the person is left living in silence, waiting for the next interruption instead of leading the melody of their own life.

Floating Staff Model

A staffing approach where direct support professionals are not assigned to a single location but instead move between multiple sites as needed, often in coordination with remote monitoring and enabling technology. This model can improve efficiency and reduce costs while maintaining quality of support.

HCBS (Home and Community-Based Services)

Medicaid-funded services that allow individuals to receive care in their homes and communities rather than in institutional settings. HCBS waivers give states flexibility to design programs that support community living.

House of CINO

The publishing and intellectual property home of the PMB ecosystem, founded by Precious "Preciosa" Myers-Brown. House of CINO develops, protects, and distributes original frameworks, digital products, tools, and editorial content across all brands, from IDD/DD resources to life alignment guides. It is the vehicle through which PMB's ideas are packaged and released to the public in accessible, scalable formats.

Hybrid Staffing Model

A service delivery approach that combines in-person direct support, enabling technology, and remote supports to provide person-centered care. Hybrid models are not about reducing support. They're about deploying support more intelligently.

ICF/IID (Intermediate Care Facility for Individuals with Intellectual Disabilities)

A Medicaid-funded residential setting that provides comprehensive care for people with intellectual disabilities. The regulations governing ICF/IID were established in 1988 and have not been fundamentally updated since.

ISP (Individual Service Plan) / Person-Centered Plan

A document that outlines an individual's goals, preferences, needs, and the services and supports they will receive. A truly person-centered plan starts with what the person wants, not what the system offers.

Liberation

In the context of enabling technology, liberation means technology that makes a person's life bigger rather than smaller. If technology increases oversight, surveillance, or constraint without corresponding benefit to the person, it is not liberating; it is controlling.

Medicaid Waiver

A provision that allows states to waive certain Medicaid requirements to provide services in alternative ways. HCBS waivers, for example, allow states to serve people in community settings rather than institutions.

Person-Centered

An approach that places the individual at the center of all decisions about their life and services. Person-centered means the person's preferences, goals, culture, and choices drive the plan. Not the system's convenience or the provider's habits.

Predictive Support

Technology that anticipates needs and risks before they become crises. Predictive support uses data patterns to identify potential problems early, allowing intervention before harm occurs.

QIDP (Qualified Intellectual Disabilities Professional)

A professional who coordinates and monitors services for individuals with intellectual disabilities. In ICF/IID settings, the QIDP is responsible for developing and implementing individual program plans and ensuring active treatment requirements are met. In HCBS settings, this role may be called something different depending on the state, but the functionality is the same. Each state's HCBS waiver application explains how this role is identified and what it is called in that state.

Remote Supports

A service framework that utilizes integrated software to connect a person with a remote team capable of responding to both the person and the assistive technology devices in their environment. Remote personnel provide real-time guidance, safety monitoring, and on-demand assistance, extending support beyond what traditional staffing alone can offer. Remote Supports are not limited to the home; the framework applies across residential, employment, and community settings. The outcome: expanded independence, privacy, and self-direction while maintaining safety, enabling people to live with support, not under supervision.

Ritmo Framework™, The

A dynamic approach to technology integration that prioritizes the continuity of care over isolated interventions. Derived from the Spanish word for "Rhythm," this framework asserts that a dignified life requires a steady, reliable beat, not just sporadic alarms. In this model, technology acts as the rhythm section, keeping the beat so the person can play the lead melody of their own life. The framework maps two parallel progressions that move in sync: the musical progression (how technology builds) and the relational progression (how life builds). The four movements are: (1) The Beat / The Individual (the single device/AT); (2) The Groove / The Courtship (the relationship and interoperability between devices); (3) The Song / The Marriage and Family (the structured Smart Home environment); and (4) The Soundtrack / The Community (the Ecosystem and Village of human support and policy that ensures the music never stops). When an ecosystem has RITMO, all four movements are in sync, and the person can live as the lead melody of their own life.

Seven Freedoms of ET™

A framework developed by Precious "Preciosa" Myers-Brown that defines the emotional and human truths that enabling technology must honor: (1) Safety Without Surveillance, (2) Choice Without Constraint, (3) Privacy Without Punishment, (4) Independence Without Isolation, (5) Identity Without Judgment, (6) Control Without Complexity, (7) Joy Without Limitations.

Smart Supports

Technology-enabled tools that enhance safety and independence while respecting dignity. Smart supports detect patterns, alert to concerns, and provide data without requiring constant human presence or visual surveillance.

Surveillance vs. Support

A critical distinction in enabling technology that comes down to mindset. Surveillance is the previous approach where monitoring exists because "we have to" or "the service coordinator requires it" or "the regulations say so" or "mom wants to know." Support is when monitoring exists because it benefits the person being served. The same technology can be either, depending on how you approach it, how you develop it, and whose data you are honoring. The mindset determines the outcome.

Tech Equity

The principle that all people, regardless of income, disability, race, language, or location, deserve access to technology that supports their independence, safety, and quality of life. Tech equity is not about having devices; it's about having dignity.

Tech Equity Triangle™

A framework developed by Precious "Preciosa" Myers-Brown that defines the three conditions necessary for technology to be equitable: Access (Can I get it?), Safety (Am I protected?), and Liberation (Does this make my life bigger?). The person, their culture, identity, dignity, and story, sits at the center.

Technology First / Tech First

A philosophy and policy approach that ensures technology solutions are considered first when determining appropriate services and supports. Technology First does not mean technology only. It means technology is part of the conversation from the beginning.

The Voice of Enabling Technology™

The professional identity and brand of Precious "Preciosa" Myers-Brown, recognizing her pioneering role in pushing the envelope in the DMV area to establish enabling technology as a distinct field within disability and aging services.

Vista Supports, LLC

A U.S.-based enabling technology transformation agency that serves as a provider to providers. Vista Supports helps IDD/DD, aging, and home-based service organizations redesign traditional services for the future of care, powered by the Vista Link™ platform, which connects devices, alerts, documentation, and routines into one ecosystem with agency-level oversight.

Vista Supports operates vendor-agnostically and works end-to-end: assessing both the person's goals and environment and the agency's operational readiness (policies, workflows, staffing, training, documentation, and risk management), then designing and implementing solutions that can be sustained at scale. Through Vista Enterprise, providers receive ongoing operational support (implementation, oversight, escalation pathways, and documentation) so remote support solutions continue to produce value-based outcomes.

Services include assessments (CAPS, ATP, ET, Medical), assistive technology and smart-home integration, procurement support, installation/configuration, workforce training, and remote supports coordination. Founded by Precious "Preciosa" Myers-Brown, Carl "Carlito" Hernandez, and Steven "Stevo" Simms, Vista Supports is women-led and minority-owned, rooted in tech equity and the belief that dignified, technology-enabled care should be available to everyone.

WATI (We Are Team Innovation) | WATI Nation™

The national community and movement advancing enabling technology across IDD/DD, HCBS, and aging services. Founded by Precious "Preciosa" Myers-Brown, WATI Nation is the fraternity of enabling technology, a no-pressure space where professionals, advocates, families, self-advocates, and innovators celebrate wins, learn together, play with cool tech and applications, and build up the movement. It doesn't matter what software or platforms you use; WATI Nation is where it's cool to talk about it. Think of it as the student union, the lounge, the tech lab, like hanging out at CES every day. This is where the movement lives and breathes.

WATI Institute™ (Workforce Advancement Through Innovation Institute)

An independent credentialing authority for Enabling Technology workforce development, founded by Precious "Preciosa" Myers-Brown. WATI Institute was born out of the practical necessities of a working provider. We built the training we couldn't find, designed to address the pain points experienced and learned from decades in the field. The Institute offers a six-level career ladder: ET-SA™ (Enabling Technology Support Assistant), CETS™ (Certified Enabling Technology Specialist), Remote-ETS™ (Remote Enabling Technology Specialist), ET-N™ (Enabling Technology Nurse), ET-PD™ (Enabling Technology Program Designer), and ET-A™ (Enabling Technology Administrator).

WATI Institute is a dynamic credentialing ecosystem for the future of support. It synthesizes the industry-shifting Technology First Framework and the evidence-based MPT Model into a practical, hands-on approach for IDD and Aging services. This program rejects "one-size-fits-all" solutions, challenging QIDPs and DSPs to act as Dignity Architects. Guided by the Enabled Life Model™, WATI credentials validate the professional's ability to use technology not just to monitor, but to radically expand a person's Safety, Freedom, and Connection.

These definitions represent a humanity-centered approach to enabling technology. Use them. Cite them. Build on them.

ABOUT THE AUTHOR

Precious "Preciosa" Myers-Brown (PMB) is The Voice of Enabling Technology™: a Transformation Strategist, Dream Technologist, and Chief Innovation and Dream Officer (CINO). With almost four decades of leadership across disability services, intellectual and developmental disabilities (I/DD), mental health, and HCBS systems, she helps providers and communities turn innovation into real-life outcomes: autonomy, dignity, safety, and freedom.

PMB is the founder of House of CINO, Vista Supports, LLC, and CINO VISTA Consulting, LLC. She helped pioneer early technology-forward service models in Washington, DC, including remote supports and remote medication processes beginning in 2006—years before these approaches became widely adopted. She is also the creator of The Enabled Life Model™, The Tech Equity Triangle™, and The Seven Freedoms of ET™: frameworks built from decades of hands-on implementation.

Certified as an Aging in Place Specialist and trained in assistive technology, PMB serves on the ANCOR Foundation Board, serves on the DC Department on Disability Services (DDS) Technology Committee, and is President of the DC Coalition of Disability Service Providers. She is also a member of the Techquity Board and the founder of the WATI Institute™, which provides specialized certification in enabling technology for disability services professionals.

Born and raised in South Jamaica, Queens (Jamaica HS…Stand UP!), PMB credits her grandmother, Francena Brown Hicks, with teaching her the meaning of freedom and the power of creating options—lessons learned over cast iron frying pans, stirring pots, and gospel humming in a Jamaica, Queens kitchen. A writer, dancer, culture lover, wellness guru, motivational speaker, and coach, PMB brings global touch to her work. Her Spanish supports cross-cultural collaboration, including organizing teams in Colombia and communicating the value of enabling technology with clarity.

Connect with Precious

All Links: links.pmbofficial.com

Website: vistasupports.com

Thank you for reading Tech Equity.

Now go build something that sets people free.

ACKNOWLEDGMENTS

No one builds a dream alone.

To my grandparents, who created space for me to be the creative I was born to be. You saw something in me before I had words for it.

To my mom, for reminding me who I was raised to be. Powerful. And as you always said, "I ain't raise no dummies." You didn't.

To Carolyn and Greg, for rolling with me every time I got my hands on new technology. Y'all never questioned it. You just showed up.

To my foundational mentors and coaches who gave me the opportunity to dream: Cindi Staib, Beth Mount, Nurse Jane from UCP, Melissa Arenas-Dewitt, and Yvette Figueroa. You saw what I could become and made space for it.

Ah, Rosita....oh let me put some respect on your name; Dr. Rosa Rivera-McCutchen for always being that example of educational excellence and homegirl.

To my roomies, Sharlane Hughes-Smith and Tasha Freeman for listening to my dreams and the constant laughs.

To my Concrete Steppas for allowing me to take this hiatus so I could finish this book!

To Cordelia Crenshaw and Acts of Random Kindness. You already know what you mean to me. Thank you for opening that door.

To Dustin Wright (RIP), who gave me the first CD showing me what this thing could look like. I never forgot.

To Donald Clark, the first person to visit the ecosystem with an open heart for innovation. Thank you for seeing what was possible.

To my first Team Innovation, for doing the thing against all odds: Ryan Tempel, Katina Cole, Eduardo Lopez-Baralt, Rainer Rodriguez-Pena, Josia Chicas, and Bonita Brown. We are still doing it.

To Arthur Ginsberg, Ashanti Kiridena, Patricia Browne, and Sandra

"Sunshine" White, for being professional supporters who encouraged me to push through when it would have been easier to stop.

To Professor Qadriyyah Johnson, for picking me up off that floor and being the reinforcer I needed. You showed up at the right time.

To Brittney Goodwin, who when I said "flip the switch" on Remote Supports during COVID, turned the whole grid on. You trusted me with everything.

To "Do it" Ian Paregol. The name says it all.

To my friends at Xandar Kardian, for trusting me with your solution.

To David Moss, for believing the dream.

To Omar Chirinos, for showing me that permission is optional but innovation is a requirement. And to the whole team at Charles Lea Center for letting me hang out with you.

To Terry Rogers, for a shared vision that led me to new spaces and brought me back to my Grandma's dream.

To Health and Joy Services, for being the first early adopters to the Vista Supports approach. For working with us to be the first Hybrid model in the DMV before anyone was doing it. You took the leap. I love you for that.

To the state agencies who invited me to the table and created space for enabling technology conversations: DC Department on Disability Services (DDS), Tennessee Department of Intellectual and Developmental Disabilities (DIDD), and Maryland Developmental Disabilities Administration (DDA). Thank you for being open and allowing me to advocate for innovation.

To the providers across the states who welcomed me and dreamed with me—New York, Pennsylvania, Oregon, Arkansas, Maine, Colorado, South Carolina, New Jersey, Missouri, Virginia, Florida, and our neighbors in Canada—thank you for trusting the vision. The best is yet to come.

To all of my board and committee members who created space for me to share this dream—the ANCOR Foundation Board, the DC DDS Technology Committee, the DC Coalition of Disability Service Providers, the Techquity Board, the Consumer Technology Association (CTA), the DC Chamber of Commerce Women in Business Committee, and the Greater Washington Black Chamber of Commerce. Your belief opened doors.

To Linda Moore, Carol Barth, Erica Smith Buchanan, Sasha Sencer, Doug Golub, and Carolyn Eaves, for reminding me that there is great value in the story and great value in preserving them to be told.

To the many people and their families I have supported over my 38 years in this work, thank you for blessing me with the opportunity to be a part of your extended family and trusting me into your inner circle. This book exists because of you.

To my partners in innovation, Carl Hernandez and Steven Simms, for seeing and believing in the Vision. We're just getting started.

To Ricardo Castiblanco-Moreno, for being my behind-the-scenes support and confidant in all of this. Eres el corazón de mi innovación.

To my international support system and family in Bogotá, Colombia. Ya sabes.

To my Travel Squad family, for holding me down.

To my sister Shanna Myers, for supporting absolutely EVERYTHING that I do. Every single thing.

To my family near and far who give me their undivided support in all my endeavors. I know it's a lot. Thank you for never making me feel like it's too much.

To Cherie Young-Simms, Shakirat Afolabi, and Tiffany Sanders, for being that continued hype squad in all my corners. Every creator needs people who cheer loud. You are mine.

To my husband, **Antonio Brown**, who is my support and my demo for everything. You let me test every idea on you first. That's love.

And to God, for trusting me with such a big dream. You don't play about me. You gave me many talents, and this book is one of your returns on investment.

I got you. I got all of you.

This is my first book. It won't be my last.